HQ
755.8
M54

C0-DWJ-080

IMPACT*

*Integrated Methods of Parent Assessment and Communication Training

E. MICHAEL LILLIBRIDGE, Ph.D.
ANDREW G. MATHIS, Ph.D.

International Marriage Encounter

2 2 3 6 0

HIEBERT LIBRARY
Fresno Pacific College - M. B. Seminary
Fresno, Calif. 93702

ISBN: 0-936098-38-4

© 1982 E. Michael Lillibridge and Andrew G. Mathis.

Printed in the United States of America. Published by International Marriage Encounter, 955 Lake Drive, St. Paul, MN 55120. All rights reserved. No portion of this book may be reprinted without permission of the publisher.

About the Authors:

E. MICHAEL LILLIBRIDGE

Dr. Lillibridge, a clinical psychologist, has been on the staff of the Counseling Center for Human Development at the University of South Florida for the past nine years. His responsibilities include individual, group, and marital therapy. He is also an adjunct assistant professor in the Department of Counselor Education and Psychology.

Dr. Lillibridge has published in the areas of communication skills training, crisis intervention and suicide, paraprofessional peer counseling, teacher training, and social effectiveness training.

Dr. Lillibridge also has a part-time private practice in marriage and family therapy.

ANDREW G. MATHIS

Dr. Mathis has been a clinical psychologist since 1958, working with children, families, couples, and individuals.

In addition to his private practice, Dr. Mathis has taught psychology and human behavior at Northwestern University Medical School in Illinois, and psychology at the University of South Florida. He conducted research with the National Training Laboratory on Human Relations Training at Bethel, Maine, and was the director of the Florida State Mental Health Clinic in Fort Pierce, Florida.

Since 1962, he has been in private practice in Tampa, Florida, where he lives with his wife and three children.

TABLE OF CONTENTS

LIST OF CHARTS

INTRODUCTION

The objective of this book is to teach you specific skills and techniques in the art of parenting. Our ultimate goal is to help you become more effective as a parent by helping you become more aware of the state of mutual respect between you and your child.

IMPACT is a program presented as a series of modules, each of which deals with a specific aspect of the parent-child relationship. Each chapter in the book will give you knowledge about parenting or will teach you a specific skill. Also included will be exercises designed to guide you in learning each skill as well as homework suggestions to help you practice what you are learning.

For more information on a 20 hour training course for parents or teachers, please contact:

E. Michael Lillibridge, Ph.D.

or

Andrew G. Mathis, Ph.D.

7804 North Florida Avenue
Tampa, FL 33604
(813) 239-3332

CHAPTER I

FOUR BASIC PSYCHOLOGICAL NEEDS ALL CHILDREN POSSESS

This first chapter is designed to help you understand four basic psychological needs. Subsequent chapters will discuss how you and your child can effectively meet these needs. Underlying these basic needs is the requirement for mutual respect in the parent-child relationship. Our most elementary assumption is that, when a child grows up in an atmosphere where mutual respect is practiced, his basic psychological needs will be optimally fulfilled. Practicing mutual respect means that each child and parent is respected in his right to achieve mastery of skill and to pursue satisfactions appropriate for his age level. When the mutual respect balance is the central focus of family life, then the likelihood of the basic needs of each family member being fulfilled is satisfactorily accomplished. Let us begin by exploring these basic psychological needs of children and parents. Then we will turn our attention to how to develop a mutual respect balance by learning how to assess Parenting Styles and acquiring effective communication skills.

A. FOUR BASIC PSYCHOLOGICAL NEEDS

Each one of us has four basic psychological needs that must be met throughout our lifetime after the requirements for food, clothing, shelter, and security are met. These four needs are:

1. The need for close, loving relationships
2. The need for autonomy and independence as a person
3. The need to achieve and be successful
4. The need for play and fun

Each of these four basic needs is with us at birth or shortly thereafter, and all four manifest themselves somewhat differently at each developmental stage of growth. For example, the loving relationship need for a newborn infant is to receive maternal love (holding and cuddling from the mother). However, the same love-need for an adolescent may be to have a parent listen and understand how he feels about the break-up of a first girlfriend relationship. The same basic love-relationship need is present in both examples but is expressed differently at different ages. As we look at these four needs, we will discuss how they appear at different ages in children.

1. Relationship Need (love)

The first need starts at the moment of birth, and it is the need for **love, attention,** and **acceptance** from the mother. Numerous studies indicate the importance of parental love for a child's successful growth and development, and even survival. In fact, young infants have been known to die if they are not given maternal love. This is true even when their physical needs (i.e., food, clothing, shelter) are sufficiently met. We now know that maternal love allows for a "bonding" to take place between mother and child, and this helps the infant to survive. At this point, love is expressed to the infant in mostly nonverbal, physical terms (i.e., holding, cuddling, carrying, and rocking the baby).

As the infant becomes a child (usually ages 2-4), the need for love is translated into the desire for parental approval and acceptance. The child still has a strong need for reassurance, contact, and support from the parent. He wants an almost unconditional kind of love at this time in his life, but during this state the child's need for acceptance is inevitably thwarted to some degree. The child's growing need for autonomy — to do things when and how he wishes — often temporarily conflicts with the child's need for acceptance when necessary limits are set by the parent. A child's need for acceptance during this stage helps him fit into your family pattern when limits and acceptance are in balance.

As the child grows older (ages 5-12), he does not require such totally unconditional support. He does, however, have two other basic relationship needs that need to be fulfilled. He needs his thoughts and feelings recognized and accepted. This is especially true when a child is experiencing a personal problem in his life. Second, in addition to wanting his parents to listen to him, the child wants to engage in positive enjoyable activities with his parents. Some of these activities could be: talking, playing games together, working on a joint project, etc. A child needs one-on-one time with each parent while doing mutually enjoyable activities.

As a child becomes an adolescent, support, acceptance and positive enjoyable time are important. But now his need for love at this stage includes not only parents but extends to peers as well. Love now becomes romantic and sexual, and many of his relationship needs are now met with boys and girls his own age. Over a period of time, his psychological development leads to forming a marriage and the cycle begins anew. So one's relationship need for love starts when born and remains throughout life. The following chart (Chart I) briefly outlines the relationship need of love at different developmental stages of children.

CHART I: DEVELOPMENTAL RELATIONSHIP NEEDS

Age of Child	Manifestation of Need
Birth to age 1	Maternal bonding, physical love (touching, holding, etc.)
Ages 1 to 3	Unconditional support, acceptance, approval
Ages 4 to 12	Listening-understanding, positive enjoyable time
Adolescence	Above needs plus peer support, acceptance, and belonging

2. Autonomy-Independence Need

The Relationship Need primarily involves love, approval, and acceptance from "significant others."* The Relationship Need is interpersonal in that it involves another person. It is usually positive and also brings people closer together. Your Autonomy-Independence Need, however, does not really involve other people in the same way as your Relationship Need. An Autonomy-Independence Need is the need to be **your own person,** separate and distinct from others. This need involves asserting oneself often against other people and expressing one's own wants and desires.

Let's examine an Autonomy-Independence Need to see how it also manifests itself at different developmental stages.

At approximately nine months of age, the infant begins to see itself as separate and distinct from other people, and is able to differentiate Mother from others. However, it is not until age 2 that the young child not only sees himself as different from other people but also begins to want to do things on his own, separate from his parents. In many parent books, this is called the "terrible twos." The child now begins to feel his own power as a person, and saying "no" or resisting parents is his way of being a person in his own right. Again, the need to be independent and autonomous is a need we have throughout life. It can take different forms at different developmental stages. At age 2, it is immature and impulsive by adult standards (with open resistance on the part of the child), but it is legitimate in that it is the first attempt by the child to assert himself as a person. As the child grows older, he usually learns to assert himself in a more ap-

---

*A "significant other" is any person with whom the individual has an ongoing relationship of importance to the individual. It can be a parent, relative, close friend, mentor, etc.

propriate manner; he becomes able to engage in independent thought and action and stand up for himself against others such as parents and siblings.

By age 4-6, the child's desire for independence-autonomy is exhibited less by simple resistance to his parents. During this period, he begins to move more toward self-exploration and exploration of his immediate environment. An interest in his own sexuality often emerges in the child at this stage. By ages 7-12, we see the child venturing, exploring, and trying to further understand the wider world around him. Doing things on his own, and acquiring a sense of mastery with projects he undertakes, help give the child a sense of autonomy and independence at this stage of development.

As the child reaches out to fill his Autonomy-Independence Need, he begins to develop a sense of who he is — his own identity. The child's sense of positive identity (the feeling that it is okay to assert himself) is formed by getting both his Relationship Need and his Autonomy-Independence Need met in some consistent way. Adolescence is a stage of development similar to the "terrible twos" where the child again begins to assert himself as a separate person in an even more resistive fashion as he prepares to break away from the family and begin a life more on his own. His striving for independence is fraught with many mixed feelings. He wants to be totally on his own and treated like an adult, but at the same time he desires the security of the family and the dependence on them. Adolescence can be a difficult time for both the young adult and the parent. Again, like the Relationship Need, your need for Autonomy-Independence is life-long. At certain developmental stages, the need for Autonomy-Independence is more pronounced, such as the "terrible twos," adolescence, and for adults the midlife transition phase. However, the need each person has for being autonomous makes him unique and different from everyone else. The following chart illustrates the developmental stages of the Autonomy-Independence Needs.

CHART II: DEVELOPMENTAL AUTONOMY-INDEPENDENCE NEEDS

Age of Child　　　**Manifestation of Need**

Birth to 2 . . . . Exploration of environment, relationship
needs very strong during this time

2 to 3 . . . . Resist parents defiantly, say "no"

4 to 6 . . . . Interest in sexual differences, intrusion into others' minds and space

7 to 12 . . . . Freedom to expand environment, learn
new skills

Adolescence . . . . . Dependent-independent conflicts

3. Achievement Need

The third basic need, Achievement, is somewhat closely aligned with the need for Autonomy-Independence. This need usually starts by ages 8-12 when a child begins to devote his time and attention to something like school achievement, a sport, or special projects, etc., where his desire is to **accomplish** something. At this point, the child wants to be good at something and gain **recognition** for his achievement.

The Achievement Need grows stronger in adolescence and in early adulthood, and is usually the basis for wanting to develop a career or occupation at which he excells. At first, the desire for achievement is fostered by his desire for social recognition and approval (Relationship Need) and, in addition, by the desire for independence as a separate person (Autonomy Need). But, as time goes on, the desire to achieve is internally motivated. The child, and then the adult, is internally motivated to achieve in order to be proficient at something, and this accomplishment becomes rewarding in and of itself. For children, this could be the desire to be a good swimmer, an accomplished saxophonist, a high achiever in school, etc. For adults, this could become the desire to be a great lawyer, a writer, a salesperson, etc. Achieving and accomplishing something — a sport, career, or project — gives him good feelings about himself and also helps build a positive self-concept in our American society.

Again, this too is a lifelong need, becoming most pronounced in adulthood. As one feels a sense of accomplishment in career goals, the desire to achieve often gets funneled into avocational pursuits. This is very true in retirement. Chart III illustrates the Developmental Stages of the Achievement Needs.

CHART III: DEVELOPMENTAL ACHIEVEMENT NEEDS

Age of Child	Manifestation of Need
Birth to 7	Focused on mastery of locomotion and manipulative skills; but focus is mainly on Relationship and Autonomy Needs
8 to 12	Mastery of projects that interest the child
Adolescence	Desire to do well at something (sport, hobby, school)
Adulthood	To become successful at something that is career- or identity-related

4. Play — Fun Need

A fourth need demonstrated by the human organism begins in childhood and remains constant throughout the life cycle. This is the need for **Fun** and **Play**. Play is something you can engage in alone or with someone else. We have all witnessed a young child absorbed in fantasy and imaginary play, carrying out the roles of several people talking excitedly to themselves. We have all probably seen adolescent girls and boys talking, laughing, or teasing one another as they flirt and joke with each other. And, as an adult, you yourself have quite likely engaged in a game or sport, socialized with friends, gone to a concert, etc. Play allows you the opportunity to relax and provides a change of pace so that you may more fully enjoy yourself and experience pleasure in your life.

Developmentally, a young child aged 1-4 normally engages in play by himself. Sharing and cooperating with other children is difficult. As a result, his most enjoyable play is usually by himself, often in the form of fantasizing with imaginary friends, or with cars, dolls, etc.

From ages 5-7, learning to play and cooperate with others becomes important. At this stage, a child likes to play with friends of his own age and usually gets along better with one at a time. Socializing in large groups is not extremely popular at this stage. In our culture, we often see girls playing with dolls and boys engaging in spacemen or cowboy-Indian games. Acting out their fantasies becomes important at this time.

From ages 7-9, children become more rule conscious during games. They often argue and bicker over the right way or wrong way to play a game. The rules to the game become very important, as rules help the child integrate his Autonomy and Achievement Needs with his Relationship Need.

As a child reaches adolescence, he begins to give up the games of childhood (where children make their own rules), and engages in adult play (with uniformly organized and externally provided rules and procedures). In adolescent and adult play, there are usually skills to lea·.ı and some expertise to be gained in playing; i.e., learning to plɛ y baseball, bridge, or riding a horse all require a learning component. Play now becomes part of his leisure time activities helping to balance out his life with the rest of his psychological needs. Chart IV outlines the Developmental Needs of Play.

CHART IV: DEVELOPMENTAL
PLAY — FUN NEEDS

Age of Child	Manifestation of Need
2 to 4	Play alone, fantasy, use of imagination
4 to 7	Play with other children, act-out fantasy
7 to 9	Rules become very important (right and wrong of every game explored)
9 to 12	More active play (games, sports, ritualistic rules)
Adolescence & Adulthood	Skills and expertise required with many activities (sports, hobbies, etc.), relaxation

Humans need the opportunity to engage in play and to experience fun in their lives. There is a multitude of activities people can enjoy, from sky diving to sitting on a park bench. The important thing is that people (children and adults) make time for fun and play both by themselves and with others.

These, then, are the four basic psychological needs of people:

1. The need for close loving relationships
2. The need for autonomy and independence as a person
3. The need to achieve and be successful
4. The need for play and fun

Your job as a parent is to help your child meet these needs in his life. If the basic needs of a child are met through the aid and nurturing of his parents, he grows and matures in psychologically healthy ways. If his needs are not met, but are frustrated and hampered, then he begins to develop emotional and behavioral problems. The goal of this parent book is to teach you skills so you can help your child meet his/her needs.

B. THE BASIC NEEDS: HOW PARENTS FRUSTRATE OR FACILITATE THE BASIC NEEDS

You have learned that all people have four basic psychological needs. In this section, you will be learning some common ways in which parents often frustrate the child in meeting his basic needs, and also you will be introduced to some general and specific ways in which you can help your child meet and satisfy these psychological needs.

1. Relationship Need

We begin with the Relationship Need (the need the child has for love, human contact, acceptance, and understanding). The most profound way you can block the Relationship Need of a child is to NEGLECT him. Simply by not spending sufficient amounts of positive time with your child, you make it very difficult for the child to get the approval, acceptance, and love he craves. When this basic need for love and positive attention is neglected, the child will seek out parents' attention in more inappropriate ways, such as getting into fights, having temper tantrums, lying, cheating, stealing, etc. In short, if neglected, a child becomes a discipline problem in order to get at least some form of attention from his parents, even if that attention is negative. For children, receiving negative attention is better than receiving no attention at all.

If neglect hampers the basic Relationship Need of love, spending positive time with the child satisfies it. We have called this positive time with children **Qualitative Time.** The constructive use of Qualitative Time is something every parent can learn. Parents and children can build a positive parent-child relationship by finding mutually enjoyable activities in which they can engage.

EXAMPLES: For a mother with a newborn infant, Qualitative Time may include holding, hugging, and talking to the child. For a seven-year-old boy, it could be a fishing expedition with his father. For a teenage girl it could be a shopping trip with her mother.

Qualitative time is one of the means parents have at their disposal in order to build a strong, positive relationship with their child. Chapter X is devoted exclusively to qualitative time, and in it this concept is further elaborated and compared with other types of time. Chapter X also presents exercises and suggestions to help parents learn this skill.

Another Relationship Need a child has is to be understood and to have his thoughts and feelings heard and accepted. This Relationship Need for feeling understood is especially true when a child is experiencing personal problems in his own life.

EXAMPLES: A child may complain of being left out of activities with the other neighborhood children; or a teenager may be hurt over the breakup of a first love relationship; a child is upset over her parents' impending divorce, etc. These examples illustrate typical problems of children. When parents ignore or do not understand, or in one way or another cut off the child without realistically dealing with his feelings about a problem, a basic Relationship Need is frustrated.

Parents need to know the do's and don'ts of effective communication to help their children when they are experiencing personal problems. Chapters III to VI will teach you the **Listening Understanding Skills** and give you instruction about specific techniques to help children when they have a problem. There are exercises, homework assignments, and rating sheets to help you learn each of these important skills. So, when the Relationship Need is met, it forms a close bond between parent and child, allows the child to experience love, and is basic for the child's development of a positive self-concept.

2. Autonomy-Independence Need

The second need is the need for Autonomy-Independence, the child's need to be his own person and have his own identity separate from others. Parents can frustrate their child's Autonomy-Independence Need in two major ways: by being OVERCOERCIVE and/or OVERSUBMISSIVE.

When parents are overcoercive or overprotective, they are restricting the child's freedom to learn from his own mistakes and grow and develop on his own. As a result, the child can become excessively dependent or rebellious toward the parent rather than becoming skilled at initiating plans or acting on his own. As the child then gets older, he may have difficulty making decisions about personal goals, occupation, friends, etc., without seeking the approval and support of others. A child who has been overprotected or overcoerced does not have the opportunity to make his own decisions and learn from his mistakes. Thus, he lacks self-confidence and then experiences anxiety when he has to undertake an independent course of action.

Another way to hinder the Autonomy-Independence Need is to be oversubmissive. This is the opposite of being overprotective and overcoercive. The oversubmissive parent allows the child too much freedom in making decisions. For young children, this is an overwhelming responsibility and they do not have the needed breadth of experience to use the freedom constructively. Over time, the oversubmitted-to child can become selfish and self-centered, having become accustomed always to getting his own way. This child makes decisions impulsively, with little thought to the future consequences of his actions. So, unlike the over-protected child who is fearful of acting independently, the oversubmitted-to child lacks self-discipline, and acts independently in an immaturely impulsive way without planning for the long-range consequences of his behavior.

What, then, can parents do to help a child deal constructively with his need for Autonomy-Independence? As you have seen, being too strict or too lenient thwarts the child's opportunity to grow and develop in his own right. Parents need to do two things to facilitate their child's Autonomy-Independence Need: first, set realistic limits for the child to adhere to, so that the child knows the definite boundaries that he must operate within; and, second, encourage and allow the child the opportunity to take graduated risks on his own, and thus learn from his own mistakes.

In Chapters VII and VIII, different types of **effective discipline** techniques for helping children are discussed. These chapters present to parents effective methods of resolving conflicts and making decisions which will help the child to successfully achieve independence and autonomy.

3. Achievement Need

The Achievement Need has to do with the desire to accomplish something, to do a task well. As a result, one will feel good about oneself and will receive recognition from others for one's work. However, parents can do two things that directly interfere with their child's Achievement Need. They can expect either too much or too little from him.

Parents who expect too much from their child are often PERFECTIONISTIC, demanding that the child achieve at a higher level than he can. Perfectionistic behavior on the part of the parents leads to two responses on the child's part. The child can overcompensate and become a super-achiever trying desperately to please his parents, or he can be "afraid to fail," and this leads to avoidance behavior on his part. Either type of response (super-achiever or avoider) keeps the child from successfully feeling a sense of accomplishment and achievement in areas he undertakes. The over-achieving child usually is "successful" at the expense of other needs (i.e., the Relationship, Fun and Play, or Autonomy Needs). The avoiding child feels inadequate and fearful of doing new things, and both types suffer from low self-esteem.

The opposite of a perfectionistic parent is one who expects or requires too little or nothing from the child. Such parents are often OVERINDULGENT, and may tend to do for the child what he could do for himself. Over a period of time, this leads to the child having little confidence in his own abilities to achieve goals on his own. This child also lacks the initiative to undertake projects and set realistic goals for himself. He often feels anxious and scared when expected to achieve something on his own.

As you see, demanding too much too soon (perfectionism) or expecting little or nothing (overindulgence) from the child interferes with his setting goals and accomplishing them successfully. Parents can do several things to help a child learn to meet his achievement needs in a more realistic manner.

First, parents need to learn skills in the area of effective parenting styles. This helps a child set limits for his own actions and teaches him that certain behaviors are expected of him. A child needs to be given graduated amounts of responsibility appropriate for his age level (i.e., chores, school work, play away from home, etc.). Chapter IX on **Parenting Styles** covers this area in detail. An additional skill parents need to learn is how to reinforce a child when he does initiate and achieve on his own. This is behavior that should not be ignored but positively reinforced. Chapter XI on **Praise** shows you how giving praise and recognition can encourage a child to succeed and achieve on his own. Parents, then, can hamper a child's Achievement Need with perfectionism or overindulgence; they can choose, instead, to facilitate the child's Achievement Need with effective parenting techniques, graduated amounts of responsibility, and lots of praise.

4. Play — Fun Need

The final need of a child is for play, to experience joy and fun in his life. A major way parents can hinder the child's need for play is simply by not allowing the child to play, and by teaching the child, through the use of PERFECTIONISM that play is a waste of time. Parents who frown on play often have difficulty allowing themselves to play and enjoy their own leisure time. Parents who don't encourage or allow their child time for play often overstress other needs, such as the Achievement Need — for example, wanting a child to do exceptionally well academically and get all A's would be overstressing the Achievement Need.

Thus, overcoercion and perfectionism can also interfere with the child's need for fun. When a child does not engage in play because of parental criticism and PUNITIVENESS, he quickly becomes unhappy and depressed and loses his zest for life. Parents need to allow and even to encourage a child to play. They also need to reinforce him for this behavior as much as they do for behavior which is connected with his Achievement

Need. Reinforcement and encouragement can take the form of parents engaging in play activities with their child. Chapter X deals with **Qualitative Time;** the section on **Individual Time** deals with learning more about this skill.

C. SUMMARY

Up to this point, you have become aware of four basic needs all people possess: (1) the need for a loving, caring relationship, (2) the need to be independent and autonomous, (3) the need to achieve and do something successful, and (4) the need to play and to enjoy leisure time. It is possible for anyone to hinder the appropriate development of these four needs, thus setting the stage for the child's development of emotional and behavioral problems.

It is also possible to encourage and facilitate these basic needs in coming to fruition. In developing the skills to do such, you as a parent will assist your child to achieve emotional growth and development.

The goal of this book is to help you identify the typical ways in which parents often hinder and block their child from meeting the four basic needs. This program will also provide you with specific skill training, in addition to acquainting you with knowledge necessary to enable you to help and assist your child in his emotional growth by meeting all of his basic psychological needs. To accomplish this twin goal, the remainder of this book is broken down into three broad areas:

1.   The first area is an assessment of different parenting attitudes and behaviors. Attention will be devoted to understanding both ineffective parenting methods and effective parenting styles, utilizing the mutual respect balance. As you read each section, you will be able to determine your parenting style. This will help you assess how well you are meeting or hindering your own four basic needs, as well as your child's needs.

2.   Second, this book presents methods which will help you learn new skills in order to become a more effective parent for your child. These skills deal with such areas as: the art of listening to children, discipline, parenting styles, conflict resolution, qualitative time, praise, etc. The extent to which you develop these skills will determine the extent to which you meet the four basic needs of your child.

3. The final area will deal with some specific problems that we have encountered in our work with parents and children. We will discuss in detail workable strategies to help you with particular problems your child might be experiencing. We have found that the majority of the problems children have can be broken down into seven basic conflict areas. We will thus focus on these conflict areas and present ways to show you how to handle them effectively.

CHAPTER II

GET ACQUAINTED WITH YOURSELF AS A PARENT — A PARENT ASSESSMENT KIT

In Chapter I, we discussed four basic needs. This chapter will focus upon how parental attitudes and behavior facilitate or frustrate the meeting of these four basic needs. It is designed to help you evaluate the type of parenting atmosphere you create in your home life, and shows you how it can be used as a guide to understanding where you may need to learn new skills to compliment your style of parenting.

We find that children grow up best and are able to meet their needs more satisfactorily when they are raised in a parenting atmosphere where the aim is to maintain a mutual respect balance between each member of the family. Deviations from this mutual respect principle will contribute to the frustration of need meeting and will heighten conflict. Regardless of the degree to which a family is in balance, there is always going to be some conflict. Thus it is important to focus our efforts upon the basic issue — namely the rights and needs of each person involved.[1]

There are six major deviations from mutual respect which parents get into called pathogens. They are: overcoercion, oversubmission, perfectionism, overindulgence, punitiveness, and neglect. The deviations will be described so that you can assess how you may have been parenting according to the mutual respect principle or to varying degrees by deviations from mutual respect.

We have observed that most of us tend to parent our children in a manner similar to how we were parented unless we deliberately have decided to follow a different pattern. Even if we have made such a decision, when we are tired, rushed for time, or not feeling up to par, we as parents tend to fall back upon reacting to our children in a manner similar to how our parents reacted to us long ago. We are fortunate when these reactions help maintain a mutual respect balance.

---

[1]For a more comprehensive description of the mutual respect principle and deviations from it, read: W. Hugh Missildine, M.D., **Your Inner Child of the Past,** Simon and Schuster, 1963.

How you were parented has been the major source of your education to become a parent. It is the "at home" atmosphere toward which you gravitate unless you decide to change it. If you realize your reactions to your child take you away from a mutual respect balance, then use this awareness to improve your relationship with your child. In any case let yourself assume, "I can change my reactions to my child in whatever ways I find appropriate." It is a painful waste of time to blame anyone, including your parents or yourself, for what has been done. Remember, it is not getting out of a mutual respect balance that does lasting harm, it is staying there that hurts and adds stress to the relationship.

A. SIX DEVIATIONS FROM MUTUAL RESPECT

In order to assist you in evaluating yourself as a parent and the type of parenting you experienced as a child, a description of the deviations from mutual respect is presented with sample statements from a Parent Inventory. The sample true-false statements as they apply to you are examples of what the Inventory is like. The Inventory itself will be made available to you if you are interested in going further. (See page 31, B. **For Further Evaluation).** This chapter will help you get a good idea of your parenting behavior on your own. What follows is an exercise in self-evaluation. Answer the true-false questions as honestly as you can.

1. **Overcoercion:**

We want so much for our children to grow up to be happy, productive people that we often find ourselves getting after them to **do** this, and **not do** that — "be good, wear your clean jeans, take your elbow off the table, don't tap your foot, chew with your mouth closed, don't sit too close to the TV, pick up your toys, hang up your clothes, wipe your feet when you come in." On we go with one direction after another hoping to instill proper habits. When they resist our directions, we go on to nag, prod, or push, trying to get them to do what we want them to do. Children need and expect a certain amount of direction. Overcoercion is directing them **too** much. It is directing and redirecting a child's activities without regard to the child's need for initiating and pursuing spontaneous interests and activities on his own. For example, when a parent does everything for the child, or tells him how to do it, because the parent does not want the child to make mistakes, to get in the way, or to take too long, etc., the parent is being overdirective. However, in order for a child to expand and develop his individuality (his

Autonomy-Independence Need) as he grows, he must have a certain amount of parental acceptance and freedom. If overdirected and overprotected, a child may respond in one of three ways:

1. The child may give up parental acceptance and resist parental overcoercion in order to expand his growing individuality (Autonomy-Independence Need) and he may be perceived as REBELLIOUS.

2. Or, the child may give up his individuality (Autonomy-Independence Need) in order to maintain parental acceptance (Relationship Need) and become quite PASSIVE and DEPENDENT.

3. Finally, a child might avoid either of these extremes and attempt to get parental acceptance or attention (Relationship-Need) and assert his individuality (Autonomy-Independence Need) by PASSIVELY RESISTING parents. This includes dawdling, forgetting, and procrastinating in a variety of areas such as chores, homework, school, etc.

Your Parent(s)' Behavior:
Answer true-false to the following statement:
"My mother/father was very bossy and dominating with me."

If you answered "true" you probably perceived your parent as having been overly directive of your activities. How you responded to your parent could have been in one of the three ways outlined above. Also, how you learned to cope with your parent may be perpetuated in your relationship with your child (i.e., you may be overcoercing your child) and this may interfere with his emerging Autonomy-Independence Need.

How You Treat Your Child:
Answer true-false to the following statement:
"I try to have people do things my way."

If you answered "true" to the above statement and your parent(s) were overcoercive with you, you might also be overcoercive with your child. This pattern can be perpetuated generation after generation. If your child is overly passive and dependent, or rebellious, or if he procrastinates excessively, you have strong clues that you may be acting in an overly coercive manner with him.

Answer true-false to the following statement:
"I tend to be more comfortable when someone else leads."

If you answered "true" to the above statement, a second possibility is that you may be quite passive with your child and spouse. You may tend to passively accept the leadership and direction of others and feel more comfortable allowing someone else to lead. You may prefer your spouse to make decisions or set limits, or to allow your child to choose what to do rather than setting limits on your child's activities when needed. You may express uncertainty by doing nothing, not deciding. Your child may thus get his way and his needs may be met at your expense.

How You Treat Yourself:
Answer true-false to the following statements:
"I actively try to please others by going along with what they think or want."
"I really have to push myself to get things done on time."

If you responded "true" to the above statements you are likely to hold back in regard to making decisions in non-routine matters. You may worry more than the average. You may procrastinate and put off doing things you think you should do. There are other routes to procrastination, but parental overcoercion is a major one. You may feel low in spirits at times because you continue to struggle with what you feel you "should" be doing rather than what you want to do. You may be overly concerned with pleasing others.

Relationship of Overcoercion with Mutual Respect:
Answer true-false to the following statements:
"My father/mother supported and helped me to build upon my ideas."
"When working with others I take an active part in decision making."

If you answered "true" to these statements you will be less inclined to feel your parent was overly coercive with you, and you will find it more natural to stay within a mutual respect balance with your child in regard to your child meeting his Autonomy-Independence Need. The likelihood of you dealing constructively with conflict and behaving in a "give and take" manner with your child or others will be enhanced. Your efforts to lead and direct your child will be less likely to result in your child feeling you are overly bossy, or that you lack interest in him, because you give your child the chance to take an active part in decision making. Furthermore, you and your child will be finding more joy in a cooperative, "at home" atmosphere.

2. Oversubmission:

Oversubmission is a deviation from mutual respect. Some parents may confuse this with giving love and security to their child. Oversubmissive parents literally become their child's servants, waiting on them and trying to comply with their every demand. When oversubmission continues over a period of time, a repetitive cycle becomes established, as follows:

1. A child is a natural-born opportunist and will take advantage of a "good thing."

2. No person or parent can be taken advantage of very long without sooner or later becoming sore about it.

3. When the parent becomes angry about being taken advantage of, the child learns to respond angrily also, to try to induce the parent, through guilt, to keep on meeting his demands.

4. The parent, out of guilt at not having been "loving," will comply — assuming this is necessary for the child's security.

5. The cycle starts again!

Once this cycle continues over a period of time, a number of behaviors may emerge in the child. These are fairly normal behaviors for preschool children: inconsideration for the rights of others, demandingness, bossiness, temper, and impulsiveness. The child is often described as "immature" when he reaches first grade, because he is not accustomed to following directions. He is accustomed to giving them. He does not easily learn to follow school routines; he does what he wants, not what the teacher is instructing him to do, such as stay in his seat, or take his turn, or do his work, etc.

Your Parent(s)' Behavior:
Answer true-false to the following statement:

"My father/mother could be talked into things easily."

If you answered "true" to this statement it suggests that your parent probably related to you by giving in to your wants and demands to an above average degree. Your parent could be talked into things easily. You may be following this model with your child (oversubmitting) because it was done to you. This may interfere with your child meeting his growing Autonomy-Independence Need.

How You Treat Your Child:
Answer true-false to the following statements:
"I tend to get into things which I later regret."
"I feel frustrated easily when I'm not allowed to do what I want."

If you answered "true" to the above statements one of several things may be happening.

1. You may find yourself in the oversubmission cycle with your child: feeling taken advantage of, uproar, guilt, more over-submission.

2. You may expect your child to comply with your paren-ting commands regardless of how your child feels, and you quickly become irritable when your child does not comply.

3. You may be avoiding the establishment of needed routines for your child, not liking to be bothered with it.

4. You may quickly grow tired of being around your child for very long at any time, because he takes advantage of you, and thus you may not give the qualitative time your child needs.

How You Treat Yourself:
Answer true-false to the following statements:
"I behave in a spontaneous, carefree manner."
"I easily feel 'fenced in' by others' expectations."

If you answered "true" to the above statements you may be impatient with yourself, expecting what you want to happen now. You may act impulsively to meet your needs and feel confined if you cannot get away from home often. Your ability to tolerate frustration may be low. You may be inclined to think that things are "awful" and that too many demands are placed on you. You may dislike being in situations where conformity or a lot of rule-following is required.

Relationship of Oversubmission with Mutual Respect:
Answer true-false to the following statements:
"My father/mother insisted that I respect the rights of others."
"I like to conduct myself around others so as to maintain a good feeling between us."

If you answered "true" to the above statements the tendency to oversubmission with yourself or others will not contribute to as much tension within yourself or between you and your child. Because of your self-respect, you will not be as inclined to oversubmit to your child's demands and you will find it easier to set limits with your child as well as consider your child's feelings in decision making.

3. Perfectionism:

Perfectionism in parenting involves the failure of a parent to accept a child at the child's current developmental level; but promises acceptance if the child's performance is beyond, and more mature than, that which is comfortable at his age level. When perfectionistic parenting is continued over a period of time, a child may react in several ways.

1. A child may continue to strive to measure up to perfectionistic parental expectations, hoping for acceptance and love. This child often becomes a super-achiever, hoping his "good" behavior will get him the desired parental acceptance.

2. A child could also become discouraged and disappointed in his performance and decide not to try. He becomes "afraid to fail" and avoids giving a task or project his full commitment.

3. Either the child who becomes a super-achiever or the child who gives up easily can become self-belittling and may develop a poor self-concept.

4. His effectiveness and productivity are eventually reduced. This applies to chores as well as school work or self-initiated projects.

Your Parent(s)' Behavior:
Answer true-false to the following statement:
  "My father/mother was difficult to please."

If you answered "false" to the above statement you probably felt your parent was not overly evaluative of what you did, or you felt his expectations of you were reasonable. He was interested in what you did and he took some pride in your accomplishments.

If you answered "true" to the above statement you may have felt that you did not receive the pleasure of knowing you measured up to parental expectations. Your parents may have falsely assumed that it was important to keep you thinking you should always do better in order to motivate you — the proverbial carrot in front of your nose. If you parent your child according to this pattern, you may have unrealistically high expectations of performance for that child, above what the child can comfortably handle and still meet his need to feel accepted by you.

How You Treat Your Child:
Answer true-false to the following statements:
  "One loses face for making mistakes."
  "I feel awful when I have not been doing things the way I should."

If you answered "true" to the previous statements you may be inclined to expect your child to achieve at a level which is discouragingly high. You may be overly concerned about what you think others think of your child or of you as the child's parent. This can add to the tendency to expect too much from your child. Perfectionism can interfere with your child's desire to feel successful and to meet his Achievement Need.

How You Treat Yourself:

Answer true-false to the following statements:

"I tend to dwell upon the mistakes I make."

"I feel ashamed to expose my shortcomings or foolish behavior."

If you answered true to the above statements you may be overly critical of your level of performance. This may interfere with your trying out new things you would like to do. You may feel others have your same high expectations of you, and thus you anticipate unnecessary criticism adding to your inner strain. Perfectionism can create tension and worry and take the joy out of doing. In the eyes of others, perfectionists are often the "successful" unhappy adults.

Relationship of Perfectionism with Mutual Respect:

Answer true-false to the following statements:

"My father/mother accepted my mistakes without making a big deal over them."

"I accept my mistakes and still look on the bright side of things."

If you answered "true" to the above statements it will help lessen the corrosive quality of any perfectionistic attitudes you may have. It implies more a capacity to pursue excellence with more tolerance for error and less a tendency to belittle or be critical of yourself or your child for a less-than-perfect performance. Furthermore, you are less likely to become discouraged at the rate of progress you (or your child) make as you work toward a goal.

4. Overindulgence:

The overindulgence pattern stems from the parent giving goods and services excessively to the child without regard to the child's needs. The oversubmissive parent waits until the child demands, then complies. The overindulgent parent initiates the giving of goods and services. The consequence of overindulgence leads the child to:

1. Continually expect the parent to spark his interest with parent-initiated activities or by being given things.

2. Become passive and bored.

3. Lack initiative and persistence, since he learns to rely on another person to motivate him and to incite his interest in something.

Your Parent(s)' Behavior:
Answer true-false to the following statement:
"Father/mother did most everything for me."

If you answered "true" to the above statement it suggests that you remember your parent(s) as tending to initiate doing things for you or giving you things frequently regardless of your need or desire for what your parent gave. This may have contributed to your learning not to initiate doing things to meet your own needs. Often a "true" response to the above statement was experienced as a form of positive regard and love from the parent, given in such a manner that it did not "spoil" you as a child nor lead to feelings of boredom.

How You Treat Your Child:

If you are parenting your child according to an overindulgent pattern (giving goods and services excessively), in addition to the three consequences listed above, your child may:

1. Have motivation and achievement difficulties in school.

2. Not have any chores at home, or if he does he is not doing them.

3. Often seem bored with play activities unless someone else is actively engaging him in an activity.

The overindulgent pattern thus leads to difficulties with the child meeting his Achievement Needs.

Answer true-false to the following statements:
"I sit around waiting for something exciting to happen."
"Nothing that I am doing interests me or turns me on."

If you answered "true" to the above statements you may be more passive in your relationship with your child because you are probably feeling the "blahs." You may rely upon your spouse to do most of the limit setting. You may rely upon your child to activate you, to get you going and doing what needs to be done.

How You Treat Yourself:
Answer true-false to the following statements:
"I am more a spectator of life rather than a participant in it."

"I do not feel as cheerful as most people seem to
be."

If you answered "true" to the above statements you are probably feeling somewhat low in spirits. Your energy level may be
low or you may not be feeling up to par physically. You may
worry a great deal about everyday disappointments or an-
ticipated loss or harm. More likely if you answered "true" to the
above statements, you may have had a significant loss which further adds to the difficulty you find in maintaining interest in
everyday tasks and activities.

Relationship of Overindulgence with Oversubmission:

Frequently these two deviations from mutual respect are both
present adding to passivity or demandingness, pessimism and a
low frustration tolerance for disappointments. Remember we
each have a tendency to gravitate in the present toward the "at
home" atmosphere of our childhood. When we do this and
begin to feel sorry for ourselves we are certain to feel low in
spirits. More realistic optimism is required, such as responding to
a disappointment with, "There went another one of life's little
tragedies — I will move on to something else with a relaxed self-
assurance."

5. Punitiveness:

Punitiveness typically involves a child who becomes the recip-
ient of parental verbal or physical aggression (criticism, severe
belittling, scolding, or spankings), often in the name of
discipline. The child usually responds to parental punitiveness in
one of two ways. The child may:

1.   Become overly cautious and self-critical.

2.   Repeatedly put himself in a position to be treated with additional punitiveness. When this happens, parents sometimes
observe that "spanking only makes him worse."

Your Parent(s)' Behavior:
Answer true-false to the following statement:
"My father/mother would put me down or punish me
for the least little thing."

If you answered "true" to the above statement you remember
that parent as having been overly critical or even harsh at times
in relationship with you when you were a child. You may have
responded in one or both of the ways mentioned above. You
find it difficult to let go or relax and have fun to meet your Play
Need.

How You Treat Your Child:
Answer true-false to the following statements:
  "When irritated I react more intensely than the event deserves."
  "I feel resentment for a long time when I have been hurt."

If you responded "true" to the above statements you may be relating at times in a punitive manner with your child. You may find yourself being overly critical or harsh with your child, afterwards realizing you were giving vent to your feelings and not responding to your child's need. Your child may be responding to you as you did to your parents when you were a child.

You may assume your child needs to learn to cope with a certain amount of harshness to get along in this world. You may find yourself frequently frustrated and on the verge of letting loose criticism toward your child. Your frustrations may not stem from any parental punitiveness from long ago but from present frustrations of your life needs. Parental punitiveness with the child can interfere with the development of close, harmonious, loving relationships, and with your child's growing need for give-and-take play activities with other children. Your child may seem sullen and depressed following punitive treatment. He also may be inclined to get into fights more frequently.

How You Treat Yourself:
Answer true-false to the following statements:
  "It is hard for me to forget when someone does me wrong."
  "I feel a desire to get even when I have been criticized."

If you answered "true" to the above statements, it is possible that you are inclined to externalize blame — to defend yourself against being "in the wrong" by holding others responsible for your behavior. This tends to anger others. If you are conscious of feeling irritable to an above-average degree, perhaps you find yourself in a particularly frustrating relationship or work atmosphere. Prolonged feelings of anger add to personal tension and stress, and can contribute to bodily pain such as headaches, GI tract problems, or the "that person gives me a pain in the neck" syndrome. Anxiety, worry, and self-belittlement often accompany feelings of anger.

Relationship of Punitiveness with Other Mutual Respect Deviations:

1. When parental punitiveness is combined with overcoercion and perfectionism, this may contribute to a stifling dictatorial

relationship with your child. This results in the child experiencing insufficient acceptance and support to develop his individuality because he is too preoccupied coping with parental encroachments. High punitiveness and perfectionism tend to intensify the higher overcoercion consequences of passivity or rebellion, or passive resistance in the child.

2. When oversubmission is combined with punitiveness, the circular pattern of oversubmission-anger-guilt and more oversubmission is often encountered.

3. Punitiveness from either parent usually has a more damaging effect upon Mutual Respect relationships for females than for males, but it damages the child regardless of sex.

4. If critical thinking is combined with high Mutual Respect attitudes, it is indicative of an above-average degree of assertiveness. This individual may enjoy debating.

6. Neglect:

Excessive neglect is the most devastating deviation from mutual respect of the six pathogens in terms of its long term effects on the developing personality of the child. It is an absence of relationships and leaves little to react to from within. When neglect is combined with other deviations from mutual respect it is different than when that is all there was — mainly a void. It is a long bleary way from infancy to adulthood when you have no one to support you and cheer you up when the going is rough, and all you do is peer into other families and wish you could be a part of them.

Neglect involves insufficient interest in or awareness of the child's need for parental attention and assistance. When a child experiences neglect throughout his developmental years, several things may result:

1. He may fail to develop inner controls, because closeness with a parenting person was lacking.

2. He tends to seek short-term satisfactions in relationships with people and becomes more impulsive in seeking gratification of his desires.

3. He may have deep, often well hidden yearnings to be loved, but he does not allow another to get close to give the love he craves. He wants closeness (to feel understood and accepted), but fears it.

Your Parent(s)' Behavior:

If you have taken the time and concentration to read this you probably did not experience excessive neglect. But you may have experienced some of it. So answer true-false to the following statement:

"My father/mother did not show interest in me or what I was doing."

If you answered "true" to the above statement, it implies that you did not have an experience of living with a significant person who gave you much interest or support as a child. The active disinterest of a parent in a child requires an adaptation by the child to the parental relationship void. Usually, this child learns to meet his needs whenever and wherever he can when neglect is present. He learns to feel "at home" without a close relationship, although he may continue to yearn for this sort of a relationship on into adulthood.

How You Treat Your Child:
Answer true-false to the following statements:
"I keep things rather distant between myself and others."
"I do not feel close to anyone."

If you answered "true" to the above statements, it may be in response to your parent(s) not showing you the interested attention you wanted as a child. You may find it difficult to spontaneously show your child the interested attention he needs. The emotional distance you experienced with your parents may be making it difficult for you to listen to your child, to give him the qualitative time he needs, and the praise and encouragement he craves for a sense of well being. These are skills you can learn to share with your child, and both of you can come to enjoy and feel enriched by having learned them.

When a child is having difficulty getting close on a feeling level, he may seek this closeness with others in fleeting ways such as hugging in a clinging manner or always seeming to yearn for more. The skills used in communicating understanding of feelings can be of special benefit to you in developing the closeness you desire and which you may sense your child is yearning for from you. The Relationship Need of children for love and understanding is the basic need most likely to be thwarted when the child is experiencing neglect.

How You Treat Yourself:
Answer true-false to the following statements:
"I go my own separate way avoiding close relationships."
"I find myself disappointed with close personal relationships."

If you answered "true" to the above statements, you may tend to think of yourself as not being "okay" or acceptable, and you may expect others not to be interested in your company. You may frequently feel lonely even when with people. Or, if someone tries to get very close to your feelings and share with you on that level, you may feel uncomfortable in this unfamiliar emotional atmosphere. You may feel a need to compensate for neglect by seeking recognition and acceptance in unusual ways by doing something outstanding yourself. You may try to compensate vicariously by desiring your child to be outstanding in some way.

Relationship of Neglect with Other Deviations from Mutual Respect:

The experience of parental neglect may be combined with parental overcoercion, perfectionism and punitiveness. This usually indicates a higher degree of distress in one's present life, and means that more work over a longer period of time is required to learn to feel reasonably comfortable in a close ongoing relationship.

7. Mutual Respect:

Mutual respect is a principle which, if followed, helps counteract or bring back into balance the possible effects of the six pathogens (overcoercion, oversubmission, perfectionism, overindulgence, punitiveness, and neglect). When mutual respect is practiced, it means that each family member is respected in his right to achieve mastery of skill and to pursue satisfactions appropriate for his age level. When a member encroaches on the right of another to do this, limits are set firmly, without belittlement so that the rights of others are insured on an ongoing basis. Some examples are as follows:

1. If you find your relationship with your child is out of balance due to your OVERCOERCION in the relationship, you may need consciously to work at being more supportive of your child's ideas and his ways of going about an activity. Granted, your way may be more efficient. But your child may not be as concerned about time as you are.

2. If your relationship with your child is out of balance due to your OVERSUBMISSION, you may need to be more firm in regard to scheduling routine activities such as chores, homework, bedtime, etc., as well as helping your child become more considerate of your rights and the rights of others.

3. If your relationship with your child is out of balance due to your PERFECTIONISM, you may need to be more accepting of his mistakes while still being optimistic with him in regard to improving his skills.

4. If your relationship with your child is out of balance due to your OVERINDULGENCE, you may need to give your child more opportunity to accept responsibility in deciding upon and initiating what he wants when he is ready to decide, instead of you trying to anticipate his wants without his active involvement.

5. If your relationship with your child is out of balance due to your PUNITIVENESS, you may need to work toward becoming less critical of his lack of expertise in expressing his feelings or doing things when and how you wish.

6. If your relationship is out of balance due to your NEGLECT of your child, you may need to work toward rearranging your priorities of time usage in order to have more time to give interested attention to your child, and to engage in mutually enjoyable activities together.

Your Parent(s)' Behavior:
Answer true-false to the following statements:
    "My father/mother focused upon my positive qualities and attributes."
    "My father/mother could give to me without requiring I appreciate it."

If you responded "true" to the above statements, it suggests that you probably feel it is natural to pursue your interests and show interested attention in your child's activities. The less your parents related to you in a mutually respectful manner, the more you may need to consciously think about and work at maintaining a mutual respect balance within your family.

Some individuals have had the privilege of a close relationship with a mentor or someone else outside the family, and have learned to work at mutual respect despite what may not have happened between them and their parents. Regardless of your parent(s)' behavior, working at maintaining a mutual respect balance within yourself (i.e., not belittling yourself) and between you and your child is what counts. How you treat your child and yourself will tell you more about this.

How You Treat Your Child:
Answer true-false to the following statements:
    "I am involved in doing many interesting things."
    "I am enthusiastically open to new ideas and proposals."

If your answers were "true" to the above statements you probably tend to act spontaneously and confidently in your relationship with your child. You actively take responsibility for including yourself in meaningful work and play relationships. If you answered "false" the more likely you are to behave hesitantly in regard to involving yourself actively with your child. "True" responses to the above statements imply that you feel joy and satisfaction from sharing in your child's life and the lives of others. You are optimistic regarding working out conflict between you and your child and about maintaining the mutual respect balance within the family.

How You Treat Yourself:

Answer true-false to the following statements:
"I try to focus on the positive in myself and others."
"I feel adequate and self-confident around others."

If you responded "true" to the above statements, it means that you actively think in a positive, confident way about yourself. You are involved in meaningful relationships and are able to make decisions for yourself. You find it natural to set limits when they are needed for yourself or others in relationship with you. In addition, you are aware of feeling the benefits of practicing mutual respect. You feel okay doing what seems right for you, despite what others may say. You do not long engage in self-belittlement; neither are you inclined to feel blue very long. The less you follow the mutual respect pattern, the more you may be inclined to think in a self-critical manner, to be pessimistic about yourself, and particularly not to like yourself or what you are doing.

Relationship of Mutual Respect to the Pathogens:

If you responded with "true" to most of the mutual respect statements it is a strong indication that you are practicing living by the principle of mutual respect. This practice helps to alleviate the discomfort implied by the deviations that lead you from a mutual respect balance within yourself or in your relationship with others. When you have been overly directive or have not set limits early enough, or have been overly critical of your child or yourself, your behavior indicated by your practicing mutual respect enables you to use a built-in guidance system to tip you off that things are out of balance. This awareness can help you not to stay there so long. It is staying out of balance that hurts, and working at getting relationships back to a comfortable balance is what enables you to appreciate your child and find joy in relationships at work and play.

If your mutual respect behavior and attitudes are low, the awareness of what is out of balance within or between you and others can be learned. Skills can be developed more effectively to practice the mutual respect way.

B. FOR FURTHER EVALUATION:

The authors have developed a Parent Assessment Inventory and have done extensive research with it since 1977 in working with individuals, families, and groups. This Inventory is designed to assist the individual in understanding his current functioning and how parent conditioning may have contributed to present behavior and attitudes. Certain parenting patterns contribute significantly to later behavior patterns and attitudes toward self and others. This chapter has been based upon research done with this Inventory as it relates to parenting one's children. The statements used to describe parent behavior and attitudes, and to describe yourself, are samples taken from this Inventory. The Inventory itself contains many more items than were used in this chapter, and therefore it can give you a more accurate picture of yourself. If you care to go further than this chapter has taken you in the self-assessment process you may contact the authors to take the Inventory and receive a computerized printout interpretation of your Inventory response pattern. The address is: 7804 N. Florida Ave., Tampa, Florida 33604.

C. SUMMARY

In Chapter I, we looked at the four basic psychological needs of your children. We pointed out that each of these needs can be frustrated or blocked by a parent's attitudes and behavior, or these basic needs can be facilitated in a positive direction by what the parent does.

The purpose of Chapter II has been to help you learn how you may be blocking your child from meeting his needs. The remainder of this book is aimed at helping you discover positive corrective measures you can take, so that you and your child can meet these basic needs.

Chart V illustrates the four basic needs and specifies which parent pathogens often block those needs; also included are the corrective skills you will be learning, and in which chapter they can be found.

CHART V: ILLUSTRATION
OF THE FOUR BASIC NEEDS

Basic Needs	Parent Pathogens	Parent Corrective Measures (Chapter)
1. Relation-ship Need	Neglect	Listening Skills (III, IV, X, XI) Qualitative Time (X)
2. Auton-omy-In-dependence Need	Overcoercion, Over-protection, Oversubmission	Effective Discipline Skills (VII and VIII)
3. Achieve-ment Need	Perfectionism, Overindulgence	Effective Parenting Styles (IX) Praise and Positive Reinforcement (XI)
4. Play-Fun Need	Punitiveness, Perfectionism	Individual Time, Qualitative Time (X)

Now, let us re-examine each need, the parent pathogens, and the necessary parenting skills to facilitate the basic needs.

The **Relationship Need** (the need for love, support, understanding, and positive time) is primarily blocked by PARENT NEGLECT (not spending sufficient enjoyable time with your child). You as a parent need to learn two basic skills to meet the Relationship Need of your child: Listening Skills (to deal with their problems and concerns) and the skill of Qualitative Time (spending enjoyable time together). The Listening Skills are explained in detail in Chapters III, IV, X, and XI; the skills for Qualitative Time are in Chapter X.

The **Autonomy-Independence Need** (the need for separateness, assertiveness, and being your own person) is primarily blocked when parents are OVERCOERCIVE or OVERSUBMISSIVE. Thus, parents can either squelch the desire for freedom (over-coercion) or allow too much of it (oversubmissiveness). Effective discipline techniques (Chapters VII and VIII) present specific strategies for dealing with a child's unacceptable behavior and at the same time help him in a realistic manner to achieve his autonomy needs.

The discipline skills do two things. First, they give YOU, the parent, specific skills to deal with a child's inappropriate and unacceptable behavior. In that sense, the discipline skills make it easier to effectively discipline your child and to meet YOUR needs. Second, effective discipline techniques help your child meet and achieve a healthy sense of autonomy by setting realistic limits on his behavior and likewise allowing him an appropriate amount of freedom relative to his age and emotional development.

The **Achievement Need** (the need to accomplish something and gain recognition from it) is most often blocked by PERFEC-TIONISM and OVERINDULGENCE. It can also be blocked by OVERCOERCION and OVERSUBMISSION. Both perfectionism and overcoercion demand and expect too much from the child. On the other hand, overindulgence and oversubmission expect too little from the child. They do for the child what he can do for himself. As a parent, two sets of skills are necessary to help a child learn to achieve in a successful manner. First, learning to give the child graduated amounts of responsibility and praising the child for accepting such is important. The when and how of PRAISE is covered in Chapter XI. Second, learning about one's parenting style and how to use it successfully (Chapter IX) helps the child deal with effective limit-setting and expectations for his performance.

The **Play-Fun Need** (the desire for enjoyment through leisure activities) is most often blocked by two parent pathogens, PERFECTIONISM and PUNITIVENESS. Perfectionism demands too much from the child and makes play either become not okay to do or become work, something to be done well or not at all. Punitiveness often means that parents are critical of anything the child does for fun, and this doesn't encourage him to play. Chapter X on Individual Time (things to do for fun by yourself) and Qualitative Time (things to do together for fun) helps you as a parent to understand the need for leisure and fun with your child.

C. HOMEWORK

1.   What are the need(s) you see in your child that need assistance from you? Check those that apply:

_____a. the need for close loving relationships
_____b. the need for autonomy and independence
_____c. the need to achieve and be successful
_____d. the need for play and fun

2.   With your knowledge of the needs listed above, and your awareness of yourself from the way you were parented, jot down what steps you need to take to help your child.

_____

_____

_____

CHAPTER III

HOW TO GIVE CHILDREN POSITIVE ATTENTION

In Chapter I, we looked at basic needs of children and how you, as a parent, can either facilitate or frustrate your child in meeting those needs. In Chapter II you explored your own parenting style. Chapter II also gave you good clues as to how you may be blocking your child from meeting some of his basic needs. For example, if you are overly perfectionistic you may be expecting too much from your child. You could be putting undue pressure on your child in his attempt to meet his Achievement Need.

The first two chapters have hopefully helped you make an initial assessment of possible problem areas in your parenting style. Now, in Chapters III through XII, we want to teach you specific skills that will help you be a more successful parent. These skills will also help you meet the basic needs we have discussed.

Chapters III through VI deal with helping children with their own personal problems. When you have skills to help a child solve his problems, then you can help the child with two of his needs: the Relationship Need and the Autonomy-Independence Need. Learning the Listening Skills discussed in the next three chapters will help you to understand your child better. This will allow you to deal more effectively with your child's personal problems and help you to form a closer and more rewarding relationship with your child. As you help your child, he will become better able to handle his own problems in an independent and autonomous way.

We shall begin by looking at some of the problems your child brings to you. Your goal will be to assist him in understanding and resolving his conflicts. The following Chapters, IV and V, as well as this one, will deal with four different Listening Skills that you as a parent can use to help your child when he is burdened by a personal problem.

A. CHILD PROBLEMS

Some typical problems that children might experience and bring to parents are:

* A 16-year-old girl says, "None of the boys are interested in asking me to the dance."

* A 7-year-old comes to you with a bored look on his face and says, "Nobody wants to play with me. What can I do?"

* A 14-year-old girl cries and wants to be left alone. She does not want to participate in activities at home or school. You know that her best friend moved away recently.

When a child has a problem, he tends to go through a four-stage process of working through the problem and sharing feelings about the problem:

1.   At first, your child will or won't risk disclosing the problem to you or someone else. You must remember that your child is concerned about how you will respond to him. Will you accept or reject him? As a general rule, people are cautious and hesitant about sharing personal problems.

2.   Once the child has decided to go ahead and risk talking about the problem, the second stage is entered wherein your child shares information and feelings about a specific problem. This usually involves discussing things like what happened, with whom, how, when, where, etc.

3.   Next — and this stage is optional, depending on the person and the problem — the child may begin to release many feelings that may have been held back for some time. The child may cry, get angry, show feelings of hurt, loneliness, etc. This stage is characterized as a catharsis or an open expression of genuine feelings. This stage is also very dependent on how you as a parent respond; the more a child feels accepted by you, the more the child will open up and share many pent-up feelings. As a result of sharing these feelings, the child usually experiences a sense of relief and will become more relaxed. If you place too much emphasis upon your child's "proper" choice of feeling words, your child will probably learn not to talk about them with you.

4.   Following this release of feelings, the child may begin to clarify the problem from a new perspective. Usually, two things happen during this last stage: (a) the child begins to understand himself better, and (b) the child finds a solution to the problem.

You as a parent can help or impede this process by HOW YOU RESPOND. If you cut off a child by what you say, you may never get beyond Stage 1 and find out what your child's real problem is. On the other hand, facilitative responses from the parent can assist a child in proceeding through all four stages and helping resolve the personal problem.

B. PARENT LISTENING SKILLS

At this point, we are going to look at Listening Skills that help your child cope with and solve personal problems. There are four Listening Skills:

Attending behavior (a nonverbal skill)
The typical helping responses
Facilitative listening
Facilitative summarization

This chapter will deal with attending behavior; Chapter IV will deal with the typical helping responses; Chapter V will focus on facilitative listening and facilitative summarization.

We are going to begin, then, with the skill of ATTENDING BEHAVIOR. This is the way in which you nonverbally present yourself to your child who comes to you with a problem. It is the first impression a child has of you and infers your interest and concern. ATTENDING BEHAVIOR MEANS GIVING YOUR TOTAL UNDIVIDED ATTENTION TO YOUR CHILD. This skill is very important because a child wants to know he has your total attention and concern. Good attending behavior strives toward this goal.

C. ATTITUDES AND BEHAVIORS

Attending behavior can be broken down into two parts: the MENTAL ATTITUDES you hold about relating to a child, and your specific PHYSICAL ATTITUDES or BEHAVIORS.

1. **Mental Attitudes.** There are three necessary attitudes which you need to have in order to be able to give someone your total attention.

First, you must MAKE A CONSCIOUS DECISION that you will give the child your individual attention for a period of time. When he comes to you with a problem, you say, "I choose to give my full undivided attention for a period of time."

Second, you need to be able to SUSPEND YOUR JUDGMENT. It is difficult to listen objectively to someone and at the same time categorize or stereotype that person. For example, if you think "My child is acting like a loser" or "He is a troublemaker" or "She'll never finish high school," you are prejudging your child. A parent needs to resist this tendency; rather, you need to attend directly to what your child is saying.

Third, the attitude you as a parent need is to RESIST DISTRACTIONS both internal and external while attending. Internal distractions are such things as letting your mind wander, going off on a tangent, or anything which detracts from the present. External distractions are those things in the environment which can distract you such as noise from another room, other children, etc. You have to ignore these things in order to attend effectively.

These three factors — making a choice to listen, suspending judgment, and avoiding distractions — are things you can decide mentally that will help you give your child your total attention.

2. Physical Attitudes

Next, we need to explore specific physical ways of demonstrating that you are attending to your child. These nonverbal behaviors are: EYE CONTACT, BODY POSTURE AND POSITION, and INTERPERSONAL DISTANCE (the actual physical distance which separates two people).

EYE CONTACT simply refers to looking at your child when he is talking to you. This can communicate several things. At the most basic level, it signals an awareness of presence, an acknowledgement of his being which is so important to him. Eye contact can be done either effectively or ineffectively. If it is too short or infrequent, or if it tends not to be intense enough, it is often ineffective. You are all familiar with the experience of talking to someone who rarely looks at you. You may find it hard to continue talking without being distracted, feeling you are imposing, or feeling that you are unimportant to that individual. For eye contact to be effective, face your child directly with a relaxed facial expression but still expressing interest and concern. You need to spontaneously look at your child for comfortable periods of time and permit your involvement to be expressed with an appropriate degree of intensity. GOOD EYE CONTACT IS A POWERFUL WAY OF LETTING A CHILD KNOW YOU ARE INTERESTED IN WHAT HE IS COMMUNICATING TO YOU.

The second point is BODY POSTURE AND POSITION. This can be defined as how you hold or position your body when you are listening or interacting with your child. This tells your child if you are physically and mentally alert, and communicates whether you are accepting or rejecting him or his ideas. Body posture as a means of attending can be carried out, like eye contact, effectively or ineffectively. Ineffective body posture is usually a "closed" body position; your body can communicate that you do not want to interact with the child at a given moment. As a parent, you may say, "I want to listen to you," but then you cross arms, legs, or turn away from, or sideways to, the child. Your VERBAL message thus indicates that you are willing to listen, but your body language indicates otherwise.

Clues which can be used to determine if your body language is closed are rigidity, or being too relaxed. In the former, a parent stiffens and gives a formal appearance and is often viewed as "uptight." The opposite — to be totally relaxed — may indicate indifference; slouching, putting your feet on the ottoman as if you would rather be napping instead of listening to the child. Another clue parents give a child is the position of their body. Positioning yourself at an angle to the child rather than facing him squarely is often interpreted by him as meaning, "I'd rather leave than stay and face you."

Good attending behavior by means of body language is indicated by an "open" rather than "closed" body position and presentation. This might, for example, include: facing the child fairly directly, not at an angle; physical alertness evident in your posture — you're not totally relaxed, yet you are not tense; you are sitting, and you may lean slightly forward and face your child; there are no body barriers (no crossed arms, no hand in front of or covering part of your face, etc.). This would be open body language, communicating your interest and willingness to listen.

The final area, in addition to eye contact and body posture, is your INTERPERSONAL DISTANCE. This involves the actual physical distance between two people facing each other. This communicates a great deal about how comfortable you feel with that person. Usually, the closer you stand to someone the more open and intimate you are willing to be. In our culture, our emotional relationships usually have a direct bearing on physical distance. With people to whom you feel emotionally close you will shorten the distance. With people you don't feel close to, you will widen the gap.

It is possible to diagram a series of invisible zones around each of us. These are known as our body zones. Imagine yourself standing face to face with someone, almost nose to nose; this zone is called the INTIMATE zone and it is usually a distance from a point of contact (touching) to about 18 inches. When someone is in your intimate zone, they are very close to you. Often, parents find that their very young children will move into their intimate zone; they feel comfortable when they are physically close (sitting on your lap or holding your hand). The second zone is the PERSONAL zone, which is from 18 to 36 inches. This is where people stand when they want to converse with you about something personal. People usually do not allow someone else into their personal zone unless they feel comfortable with them. The third zone is the SOCIAL zone, ranging from 3 to 5 feet. This is where most social and conversational interactions occur. The last zone is the PUBLIC zone, which starts about 5 feet from us. This is where you feel comfortable with strangers.

We must remember that the above zones are only estimates that vary with individual differences, cultural differences, sex, or a change in mood or relationship. The point to be made is that ALL of these zones occur in all people and the distance we stand or sit from anyone has an impact on the relationship.

Ineffective attending behavior via interpersonal distance occurs if you are either TOO CLOSE or TOO FAR away from the child. In other words, if you are too close to the child (in his intimate zone) he may feel intruded upon. If you are sitting too far away (for example, sitting 10 feet away) while a child is trying to talk about personal problems, he may very well feel you are not interested in him. An appropriate or effective interpersonal distance involves finding a distance comfortable for both of you. Generally, children like to be in the personal zone when discussing a problem. A small child likes to be in our intimate zone. It is important with a small child to maintain a sense of closeness. To do this, you must get down to his level by sitting down or kneeling near him.

The greatest impact in attending behavior is when you attend in all these areas at one time: eye contact, body posture, interpersonal distance. An example of this might be sitting, facing a child directly while looking at him, leaning slightly forward at a comfortable distance, choosing to give your full attention, suspending judgment, and avoiding distractions. Attending behavior is a method of mentally and physically giving your child your total, undivided attention.

D. **REMEMBER:** ATTENDING BEHAVIOR MEANS GIVING YOUR TOTAL, UNDIVIDED ATTENTION TO YOUR CHILD.

The following chart outlines the different and specific attending behaviors:

CHART VI: ATTENDING BEHAVIORS

Mental Attitudes	Physical Attitudes
1. Deciding to listen	1. Good eye contact
2. Suspending judgment	2. Open body posture
3. Avoiding internal/external distractions	3. Appropriate interpersonal distance

Attending behavior has two major benefits: one for you the parent, and one for the child. ATTENDING aids the parent in following and understanding the child's comments, thus the better you actually hear and understand what the child is trying to communicate. The more you train yourself to be an effective attender, the better listener you become.

Attending behavior also aids your child. When a child knows someone is really listening, he finds it easier to organize his thoughts and feelings. Thus, the child expresses these more effectively. When your child senses your interest and attention, he feels cared for and valued. Attending behavior is a very powerful nonverbal skill that gives your child the message that you are interested in him.

E. SUMMARY

In conclusion, when you are not attending to a person, that person tends to have difficulty in communicating feelings. A child will become sidetracked by your inattentive behavior and often has to try to gain your attention rather than being able to focus on himself and his problems. With effective attending behavior, a child can usually formulate his thoughts, feelings and ideas, and present them in a clear manner. Your demonstration of good attending behavior thus helps the child to express and articulate his problems better.

While your attending behavior communicates concern and interest to the child with problems, more must be done in order to help him in his distress. You need to prove you hear him and understand him by responding verbally as well as nonverbally. The next two chapters (IV and V) look at the verbal skills of helping.

F. HOMEWORK

A good homework assignment for attending behavior is: first, try NOT attending to someone. Don't look at the person, don't face him squarely, consider sitting too close or too far. Have some closed body position(s) or movement(s). Do this for two or three minutes while someone is talking to you. Find out what the effect is.

Then try effective attending behavior. This time, face the person directly, maintain good eye contact, sit or stand at an appropriate distance, give your full and undivided attention.

What is the difference in results of these two experiments?

CHAPTER IV

HELPFUL AND HINDERING TALK WITH CHILDREN

Attending behavior has set the stage for the helping counseling process. Now it is time to look at some common verbal responses all parents make to help a child when he has problems. It has been found that there are FIVE TYPICAL WAYS of responding that most parents use when they want to help their children solve a problem. Before these typical parent responses are explored, it is important for you to become aware of how you as a parent respond to a child who is upset. Listed below are 3 problems. Read each statement, and WRITE WHAT YOU WOULD SAY TO THE CHILD IF HE/SHE WERE ACTUAL-LY TALKING TO YOU (Remember, write in word for word what you would say for each example.)

1.   Your 14-year-old boy comes home from school and says to you, "I hate school, I can't stand it; it's all dumb. I can't stand all of that garbage teachers dish out. It doesn't make any sense to me." RESPONSE OF PARENT:

_____

_____

2.   Six-year-old Tyler says, as he enters the house, "The big kids won't let me play with them. They want to play their games and they won't let me play," (starts to cry). RESPONSE OF PARENT:

_____

_____

3.   Sixteen-year-old Linda comes home after a school dance, crying, "No one wants to dance with me. It's because of my face, it's all broken out. I hate it. I'm horrible-looking!" RESPONSE OF PARENT:

_____

_____

A. FIVE PARENT RESPONSES

Now read the following section on the FIVE TYPICAL WAYS parents usually respond, and try to categorize which response style(s) you used in the above exercise. The five typical helping responses are:

1. Questions
2. Advice
3. Support and Reassurance
4. Praise
5. Using Logic or Rational Arguments

These are the most common responses that everyone (including parents) uses when trying to help someone with personal problems.

As parents, you have two goals here. The first is to learn which of these five typical responses you use most of the time. For example, do you ask QUESTIONS when your child comes to you with a problem, or are you more likely to give ADVICE when he comes to you for help? Your second goal is to evaluate the effectiveness of these five responses when you use them. Sometimes these typical helping responses help a child to resolve a problem. However, sometimes they can do just the opposite. They can hinder and interfere with the child's ability to solve a problem. They can cut off communication between parent and child, and can even make the problem worse.

If the five responses sometimes make a problem better and sometimes make it worse, how do you as a parent know when to use them and when not to? It has been found that a child will give you very specific clues as to the effectiveness of your responses. For example, if he finds your advice helpful, he will respond with specific clues which say that advice is what he was seeking. If, on the other hand, the advice was not helpful, the child's verbal and nonverbal clues will reflect this. CHILDREN ALWAYS GIVE CLUES TO TELL YOU IF YOUR RESPONSES OF ADVICE, QUESTION, SUPPORT, LOGIC, OR PRAISE ARE HELPFUL OR NOT.

In the following section, the five typical parental responses are presented with an eye to helping you determine when and why they are sometimes helpful and sometimes not. In addition, the clues to look for will be presented for each helping response. Read the following section describing typical helping responses, determine which of the five you use most frequently, and learn the clues which are necessary to evaluate each response's effectiveness.

1. **Questions**

Questions are one of the most common responses a parent uses to deal with his child's problems. Questions refer to asking for specific information about a person, situation, or problem. Examples: "Why did this happen?", "Who were you with?", "Where were you?", "Did you talk to the teacher about it?"

A. WHEN QUESTIONS ARE NOT HELPFUL

Questions may be useful for getting information but they often won't work as a counseling skill because they "derail" a child, throw him off, or take him away from the direction he intended to go. For example, your child says he doesn't like school and you guess there may be a problem with the homeroom teacher. As a result, you ask a lot of questions about how he gets along with this teacher. However, the child may not like school because he is having trouble getting along with other kids. Thus, you have "derailed" the child by your questioning.

In addition, children often tend to resent questions, or they wonder why you are asking specific questions. Questions also give the impression that you will be able to give the child the right answer to his problem if you can just get enough information. This may not always be possible.

A good clue to determine if questions are blocking rather than facilitating communication is when a child simply answers your questions — perhaps with short, abrupt answers — and doesn't open up further. This is an excellent clue showing that your questions are not helpful and may be derailing him. Another clue to the problem of determining the worth of a particular question is if you find yourself not listening to the child's responses but rather thinking about your next question. This should warn you that your questions are not really helping your child at that point.

B. WHEN QUESTIONS ARE HELPFUL

Questions are at times helpful to the child who has a problem. For the child who feels confused and lost, questions help draw information out of him and sometimes allow him to perceive a general pattern or solution to the problem. When questions occur, the child will usually answer them, but not always spontaneously provide additional information. A clue to successful questions is when the child opens up and shares information freely about himself. When questions are helpful and facilitative, details are spontaneously and freely given. So, when children open up and give more information than you asked for in some detail about their problem, you can ascertain that your questions are being helpful.

2. Advice

Advice or giving suggestions is providing the child with your solution/idea/method of resolving his problem. Examples: "Why don't you try this," "You would be better off if you did this," "I have an idea; why don't you..."

A. WHEN ADVICE IS NOT HELPFUL

Advice often does not help because it can be premature. You may be giving advice to a problem which the child has presented but which is not the real problem. Advice often does not allow the child the chance to attempt to resolve the problem on his own. Finally, advice is often the result of your ANXIETY in an attempt to find a quick solution, so YOU will feel better.

The way to find out if advice is helpful or not is to listen for certain clues. If a child openly rebels against advice, it will usually be in this form: "I don't think that will work," or "Yes, but..." or "What if..." YES BUT means that the child is saying he likes your ideas or suggestions but that he thinks that for some reason it won't work for him. WHAT IF means that the child is challenging your ideas, asking you to prove that they will in fact work. If a child repeatedly responds with YES BUT or WHAT IF, your advice or suggestion probably won't work and will impede him from solving his problem. In addition, a child may covertly respond to unwanted or unbelievable advice with silence. This is his way of saying, "I do not feel up to or ready to do what you propose." He may experience your advice as a form of overcoercion and respond with silent passive resistance.

B. WHEN ADVICE IS HELPFUL

Sometimes advice can be helpful, especially if the child is ready to hear it and it is a solution that fits his needs and style of behavior. A child is often so upset or involved with a problem that he has not perceived some obvious and effective solutions. A clue that advice is helpful is when a child has a LIGHT BULB experience: "I never thought of that," or "Why didn't I think of that; it's a great idea!" In such cases, your idea has provided a solution that meets the child's needs.

But, remember to listen to your children's clues. Open resistance (or YES BUT or WHAT IF) are strong clues that advice will backfire if repeatedly used. On the other hand, the LIGHT BULB experience means that the advice given is very helpful and facilitative.

3. Support and Reassurance

There are two types of support and reassurance messages that parents often use: although things are bad now, they will get better in the future; and, I've had the same problem (responses where you disclose how you feel). Examples are: "Things will look better tomorrow, you'll see." "Boy, I had a problem like that; here's what I did."

A. WHEN SUPPORT/REASSURANCE IS NOT HELPFUL

Support and reassurance often do not work because they convey to a child that you want him to change, that you don't accept his feeling at that given moment. Also, a child often feels you do not understand him when you use reassurance. Finally, if your support and reassurance do not work, a child may feel you have misled him. Again, there are clues to tell you whether support and reassurance are being helpful or harmful. The child will sometimes openly resist and argue with you, or express behavioral or verbal frustration. A common reaction to reassurance is: **"But you don't understand!"** This is a strong clue that a supportive response is at that moment not helping the child.

B. WHEN SUPPORT AND REASSURANCE ARE HELPFUL

Sometimes support and reassurance are helpful. The child feels relieved and realizes he was being too pessimistic or was seeing the problem with too narrow a viewpoint. Reassurance and support make this child feel that there is hope and the chance for a positive outcome. He will usually give verbal clues indicating support and reassurance are having a beneficial effect: "Yes, I guess you may be right; things will probably get better." Again, listen for the clues.

4. Praise

Praise refers to making positive judgments or evaluations about a child or about something he has done or experienced. Examples of positive evaluation are: "You really are bright and intelligent; don't say you're not." "You can make friends easily; you're so sociable."

A. WHEN PRAISE IS NOT HELPFUL

If your child is really upset, saying positive things can backfire. The child may not feel as good as you expect and may argue with your positive evaluation. For example: "I'm not smart, I'm dumb. I can't do this school work, it's too hard for me." Many children do not like others to make evaluations about them, especially evaluations which are different from their own. A child who feels dumb at a given moment is often not at all reassured by a parent's praise. When praise is not helpful, the clue is generally that the child will ARGUE or DISAGREE. In such cases, the praise will not help him solve his problem.

B. WHEN PRAISE IS HELPFUL

Evaluations can be helpful if they concur with the child's self-perception. For example, a child who feels he is bright is not usually put off by a parent's remark of: "You're such an intelligent young man," because it concurs with his self-perception. The clue to the effectiveness of praise is how the child responds. If the child ACCEPTS your compliment, praise tends to be helpful and will make him feel better. Again, remember to listen to the clues to evaluate the effectiveness of your praise and compliments.

5. Logic

Logic and rational arguments refer to a disagreement with the child's perception of the problem. This can be done calmly and rationally, or heatedly and argumentatively. Examples: "The facts are these." "Yes, but..." "Here is why/where you are wrong..."

A. WHEN LOGIC IS NOT HELPFUL

A child often feels inferior or put down by the use of adult logic. It can provoke counterarguments from the child, leading to disagreements and conflict rather than to a solution to the problem. REJECTION or RESISTANCE to the parent's argument is a clue that logic or rationality should not be used at that time. They are not helpful at that point.

B. WHEN LOGIC IS HELPFUL

If logic or rational argument is to be effective, the child must understand the point the parent is making, and agree with it. Example: A 15-year-old hates school and is thinking of quitting. The parent might respond with: "High school graduates get better jobs than those who quit before graduation." The child must accept the accuracy of the parent's position for logic to be effective here. The clue will be that the child ACCEPTS your point of view, if logic is being helpful. A child is most likely to accept your point of view if your arguments are something he has not thought of, if you present them in a calm and rational manner, and if any hurt, pain, or hostility has been vented beforehand.

Chart VII summarizes the typical parent responses and the frequent clues determining whether they are helpful or not. It is important to be sensitive to the effectiveness of your "helping responses." So, listen to the clues. Your familiarity with the clues presented directly affects your ability to correctly perceive the effectiveness of your responses.

CHART VII: CLUE SHEET

If you are not helpful	If you are helpful
QUESTIONS: Resistance — Child says little (yes/no/brief information); derailing.	The child opens up, shares information spontaneously
ADVICE: Open resistance — "I don't need that"; subtle resistance — "Yes but," "What if."	Acceptance: light bulb experience; "I never thought of that"; "Okay, I'll try your idea."
SUPPORT AND REASSURANCE: Open resistance — child argues with you; subtle resistance — "But you don't understand."	Acceptance: "Yes, maybe you're right; things will get better."
PRAISE: Resistance — "No I'm not an intelligent person"; child feels manipulated — "You're just saying that to keep me in school"; child feels misunderstood — "But you don't understand."	Acceptance: "Yes, I agree." Non-verbal agreement.
LOGIC AND RATIONAL ARGUMENT: Open or subtle rejection; counterarguments from the child.	Agreement: "Yes, I see your side of it; I think you have a point."

Before going on to the next chapter, return to page 43 where you wrote in your responses to the three problems. Now analyze your responses, and see if they are among the five typical responses or some combination of the five.

B. SUMMARY

In summary, these five responses (QUESTIONS, ADVICE, SUPPORT, PRAISE, LOGIC) are most often used by parents, and everyone else for that matter, to help people when they have problems. Sometimes they work, and sometimes they don't. If they work, use them; if not, don't use them.

The clues children give you are the key to evaluating whether the five typical responses are helpful or not helpful.

C. HOMEWORK

The next time your child has a problem, choose one of the typical five responses. Repeatedly use it, and look for the clues that determine whether your response is helpful or not helpful.

CHAPTER V

WHY FACILITATIVE LISTENING WORKS

We have looked at the most common ways parents respond to a child when he has problems. Sometimes these typical helping responses do not work. Therefore, we will examine a sixth way of responding, called **Facilitative Listening,** which can be very helpful toward finding solutions to a child's problems.

A. FACILITATIVE LISTENING

People in the helping professions have realized for a long time the benefit of "tuning into" the feelings of a person as a way of assisting in dealing with and resolving problems. The concept of "reflection of feelings," developed by psychologist Dr. Carl Rogers, is a way of responding to a child facilitatively.

Facilitative Listening is a technique or skill which enables you, the parent, to communicate your caring, concern, and acceptance by attempting to see the world through your child's eyes. It is an attempt to get "into the skin" of the child and experience the world as perceived by that child at that moment. As this empathy is demonstrated by your verbal feedback or Facilitative Listening, the child with a problem is able to express and explore feelings and go through the process we presented at the beginning of Chapter III. That is, taking the risk to discuss his problem, expressing his feelings, and then understanding himself better and finally finding a solution to his problems.

Let's move from a general definition of the skill of Facilitative Listening to a specific operational definition. Facilitative Listening is composed of two parts: (1) the parent must be able to accurately understand the child's feelings, and (2) the parent must be able to demonstrate this by accurately restating the feelings back to the child. Here are some brief examples to illustrate the process of Facilitative Listening:

CHILD (angry): "I hate school; it's nothing but a lot of garbage! I'm not learning anything!"

PARENT (Facilitative response): "You're really fed up with school and you're angry. You are not getting what you want."

CHILD (discouraged after moving to a new city): "Things are really rough here; I haven't met any new people and all I do is sit inside all day."

PARENT (Facilitative response): "You're really lonely as a result of having no close friends to play with."

In both examples, the parent attempts to listen to the child and then gives feedback on how he feels. A necessary part of the skill of Facilitative Listening is to realize that there are several parts to a child's communications. First, there is the INTENDED-FELT COMMUNICATION. This means how the child feels, what's going on inside. Second, there is the EXPRESSED COMMUNICATION. This is what the child actually says to you. Finally, there is the RECEIVED COMMUNICATION, and this is what **you** hear. Facilitative Listening is not focusing on the expressed communication but focusing on the intended-felt communication. So, rather than focusing on the words, you are trying to focus on the feelings behind the words. Chart VIII illustrates this process of Facilitative Listening.

CHART VIII: FACILITATIVE LISTENING

Child   **Parent**

1. Intended-Felt Comm. + 2. Expressed Comm. = 3. Received Comm.

(What the child feels   (What the child says)   (What the parent
inside)   hears)

⬆   ⬆
         (Feedback of what parent hears)

It is not easy to determine what the child really feels just from the expressed communication (words). However, since Facilitative Listening focuses on the intended-felt communication, it is necessary to try to see beyond the purely verbal message. It may help to realize that expressed communication is made up of three parts: (1) the ACTUAL verbal message (what the child says word for word), (2) the PARAVERBAL message (how the child speaks, voice tone, inflection, timing of words, etc.), and (3) NONVERBAL messages (a child's body language). So there are three channels of communication which will help you determine what the intended message is and which will give you clues as to how the child feels. Chart IX illustrates this:

CHART IX: MESSAGE CHANNELS

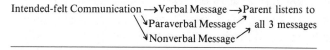

The following example illustrates these three channels of communication. An adolescent says to you: "My girlfriend left me." Just from the words alone (the verbal message), you don't know how the child really feels. He could feel angry, sad, or even happy. So you have to listen to the paraverbal message (voice tone, inflection of words) and the nonverbal message (body posture) to determine how the child feels inside. In the paraverbal message, if the voice is shaky and if in the nonverbal message the adolescent has his head down and is teary-eyed, you could conclude that the girlfriend's leaving him is upsetting and distressing to him.

CHART X: EXAMPLES OF CHANNELS OF COMMUNICATION

Verbal: "My girlfriend left me."
Paraverbal: Shaky voice.
Nonverbal: Head down, teary-eyed.

So it is not just the verbal message alone, but the verbal, nonverbal, and paraverbal messages combined that tell you how a child is really feeling.

Consider another example of a child with a problem who has a parent who uses Facilitative Listening. In this example, the parent listened to the feelings behind the words and also relied on the paraverbal and nonverbal messages to get at those feelings. The following excerpts demonstrate the Facilitative Listening technique used with a high school youth having difficulty relating to people:

CHILD: "I haven't been able to get any studying done; I'm always getting into hassles with Bill" (his older brother).

PARENT: "You seem pretty upset by all this."

CHILD: "Yes, I guess I am. I never get my studying done; he always has his friends over. They're horsing around or doing something all the time. It's impossible."

PARENT: "You're really frustrated by all their behavior and don't know just what to do."

CHILD: "He doesn't care about me at all. I have to study. I need to get good marks this year to bring up my grades."

PARENT: "You are really angry at him."

CHILD: "Yes, he makes me mad. He and all his friends are just fooling around; I don't get any work done. Bill has more friends than you can shake a stick at!"

PARENT: "You sound a little envious."

CHILD: "Well, maybe; he has lots of friends who are over all the time, and he dates a lot. It kind of gets to me — all those girls."

PARENT: "You're kind of jealous of his ability to get girls."

CHILD: "I guess so. I don't seem to be able to make friends as easily as he does, especially with girls. He's always getting dates."

PARENT: "And you're kind of confused as to how to go about getting dates."

CHILD: "Sort of. I'm just not sure what it takes."

PARENT: "You have some doubts about your ability?"

CHILD: "I do. I'm afraid to ask girls out, or even to talk with them sometimes."

PARENT: "It's really hard for you to relate to people, especially girls. You're afraid you might get rejected."

CHILD: "Yes, that's it."

From this example, you see the parent has not just relied on the words spoken by the child to determine how he feels, but also listened to paraverbal and watched for nonverbal aspects of the message. The process of Facilitative Listening tunes into the feelings of a child moment by moment, as he speaks. This process allows him to explore and understand himself better, and many times will lead him to solve his own problems.

The next two exercises are designed for you to practice the skill of Facilitative Listening. The first exercise contains statements by children. You are to determine three things from each child's statements:

1. How would you rate the child's feelings?
   A. Are they positive (happy, delighted)
   B. Are they negative (angry, depressed)
   C. Are they mixed (excited, but also scared)

2. What is the specific feeling expressed? (anger, hurt, confusion)

3. Make a complete sentence restating the feeling.

EXAMPLE: MARY (12 years old) says, "It's that Mrs. Jones. I can't stand her, and she's got to be my teacher for the whole year!"

1. Circle one: positive **negative** mixed

2. Feelings: **anger, frustration**

3. Response: **"You're stuck with her for a long time and it's frustrating."**

EXERCISE A

JOHNNY (7 years old) says: "None of the kids want to play with me. They told me to go away. That's not fair!"
1. Circle one: positive negative mixed

2. Feelings: _____

3. Response: _____

ELLEN (5 years old) says: "I don't want to go to the doctor because I will have to get an allergy shot."

1. Circle one: positive negative mixed

2. Feelings: _____

3. Response: _____

TIM (14 years old) comes home, saying: "I got an A in history! I can't believe it; I thought I was going to get a C."

1. Circle one: positive negative mixed

2. Feelings: _____

3. Response: _____

RON (15 years old) says: "If Dad says one more thing about the way I keep my hair, I'm going to let him have it!"

1. Circle one: positive negative mixed

2. Feelings: _____

3. Response: _____

ROBERT (9 years old): "I really like to play ball with Roger, but he gets mad and hits me."

1. Circle one: positive   negative   mixed

2. Feelings: _____

3. Response: _____

SCORING KEY:

JOHNNY:
1. Negative
2. Hurt, rejected
3. "It's really tough to be shoved out by other kids."

ELLEN:
1. Negative
2. Fear
3. "You're afraid to go to the doctor because the shot will hurt."

TIM:
1. Positive
2. Surprised, happy, confused
3. "You're pleased but you didn't expect it, did you?"

RON:
1. Negative
2. Anger, fed up
3. "You're fed up with his criticism; you've had it."

ROBERT:
1. Mixed
2. Confused, not sure what to do
3. "You're not sure what to do. You like Roger's company but you're not sure if it's worth the price of getting hit."

EXERCISE B

In the next exercise, there are more statements by children with problems. This time, write in the Facilitative Listening response and compare your answers with the Scoring Key, below the exercise.

1. Matt (9 years old) takes away 7-year-old Roberta's toy when playing outside. Roberta comes crying to you, saying: "Matt took my toy!" Response: _____

2. Ronnie (8 years old) says: "I hate Susie. I wish she didn't live here. You are always talking to her and helping her with homework assignments." Response: _____

_____

3. Steve (9 years old) comes home saying: "There's nothing to do. Nobody to play with. Jimmy's not around and Bobby is home sick. What is there to do?" Response: _____

_____

4. Sheryl (17 years old) says: "I can't believe it. Ron Jones asked me out! He's quarterback on the football team!" Response:

_____

_____

5. Donna (16 years old) says: "I want to drop Glee Club. The music teacher wants us to practice all the time — it's too much!" Response: _____

_____

Now compare your answers with those in the scoring key.

SCORING KEY:

1. You're really mad at Matt.
2. It doesn't seem fair; you feel I don't care enough for you anymore.
3. You sound bored and lonely.
4. You're thrilled. This is something you have been looking forward to.
5. You're pretty frustrated; the teacher expects too much of you.

B. FACILITATIVE SUMMARIZATION

The fourth skill to be used when a child has problems is **Facilitative Summarization.** Facilitative Listening means tuning into the feelings and experiences of the child as he expresses these feelings from moment to moment. At the end of a Facilitative Listening interchange, you may wish to summarize or try to pull together everything you have heard. This is what is called Facilitative Summarization. It is the same as Facilitative Listening, but you will pull together and express the OVERALL message the child gave you.

In essence, you will be "condensing" or "crystallizing" the important things you have heard. For example: An adolescent may talk for half an hour about the breakup of a romance, as well as problems with school and work. You might respond: "If I'm hearing you right, the fact that your girlfriend left you has caused a lot of problems with school, your friends, and even work. That relationship was very important to you." If you summarize accurately, you get agreement from the child that you understand the problem and, even though he has talked about a number of issues (school, friends, work), your summarization has put these in perspective. In this case, the breakup of the romantic relationship has added stress to his daily life, contributing to previously unexperienced problems.

Facilitative Summarization helps you AND the child. It helps the child clarify his feelings by helping him pull the various things you have discussed together into a compact, more easily understood package. In short, it aids him in understanding himself. It also helps you make certain that you are following the MAIN THEME of the message. Facilitative Summarization is a transitional skill: If you want to go on to some problem-solving for the child, summarization will be important to the process. (The next chapter will cover problem-solving in detail.)

C. **SUMMARY**

In summary, in Chapters III, IV, and V, you have looked at four important skills to use in helping children when they have problems:

1. Attending Behavior
2. Typical Helping Responses
3. Facilitative Listening
4. Facilitative Summarization

These skills help define the problems and deal with a child's feelings, with an eye to helping solve the problems. The next chapter pulls these four skills together and shows you how to integrate them into a comprehensive helping process.

D. **HOMEWORK**

Spend the next week doing a self-assessment. Find out which of the five typical helping responses (questions, advice, support and reassurance, praise, logic) you use most often. Also, listen for clues and feedback from your child so that you can test the effectiveness of your responses.

Second, practice Facilitative Listening. This is probably a new skill for you. Using it with your child as often as possible will help you learn it faster.

CHART XI: CHECKLIST FOR LISTENING SKILL PRACTICE

	Able to Use Skill Appropriately	Used Skill Inappropriately or Not at All
ATTENDING BEHAVIOR		
Good eye contact	_____	_____
Open body posture	_____	_____
Appropriate closeness	_____	_____
TYPICAL HELPING RESPONSES		
Questions	_____	_____
Advice	_____	_____
Support/Reassurance	_____	_____
Praise	_____	_____
Logic/Arguments	_____	_____
FACILITATIVE LISTENING		
Accurate statement of feelings	_____	_____
FACILITATIVE SUMMARIZATION		
Expression of feedback	_____	_____
Essence of message	_____	_____

CHAPTER VI

SIX STEPS TO SOLVING CHILDREN'S PROBLEMS

A. SIX HELPING STEPS

The previous three chapters explored four sets of Listening Skills which parents can utilize to help a child when he is troubled by a problem. Now it will be necessary to incorporate those skills into a comprehensive model. Chart XII is an outline of a helping process paradigm and provides a model for working with a child who has a problem. The following six steps can be used by parents to help a child in distress. You can use some or all of these six steps in a particular situation.

CHART XII: HELPING PROCESS PARADIGM — SIX STEPS

(1) Attending Behavior	(2) Facilitative Behavior	(3) Facilitative Summarization
		You have three choices at the completion of this Step. a. Stop! Child solves problem. b. Go back to Step 2, then proceed. c. Go on to Step 4.

(4) Parent Initiated Responses	(5) Facilitative Listening	(6) Implementation
a. Parent Self- disclosure b. Typical Helping Responses 1. Advice 2. Questions 3. Support 4. Logic 5. Praise c. Brain Storming		

Step 1: Attending Behavior. Your first step in assisting your child is attending to that child, giving him your TOTAL PSYCHOLOGICAL ATTENTION. You do this by use of eye contact, body posture, and interpersonal distance, along with an accepting and non-judgmental attitude.

Step 2: Facilitative Listening. This step involves your tuning in to the child to hear what he is feeling and expressing, so you can restate or clarify thoughts and feelings. Facilitative Listening allows your child to explore feelings and thoughts in depth and to gain satisfaction from releasing pent-up feelings, clarifying thoughts, and defining personal situations in a new light.

Step 3: Facilitative Summarization. At some point after you have spent time with Facilitative Listening and you believe you have heard the child's real feelings and thoughts on a specific subject, you may try to summarize those feelings and thoughts, restating them based on how you interpret the child's message. This step allows the child to crystallize his feelings and perceptions about a problem. It also helps you as a parent to check out whether you have fully understood the problem your child is expressing. As a result of Facilitative Summarization, one or more of three things takes place:

a. The conversation or dialogue ends: A child has discussed the problem and via the parent's Facilitative Listening and Summarization gains a better understanding of the problem. The child feels ready and willing to stop. He may feel a sense of relief and catharsis and have new insights and understanding. He may also come up with a solution to the problem and decide to implement it.

b. A second alternative, as a result of summarization, is to go back and do **more facilitative listening.** This is a process that often happens as you accurately summarize a person's experience. This leads to the child exploring the problem in more depth or examining new problem areas of importance. This step (Facilitative Listening — Summarization — Facilitative Listening, etc.) may be repeated many times in the course of the helping process.

c. A third alternative after Facilitative Summarization is to move on to **more action-oriented approaches.** When this happens, you clearly understand the problem and wish to move in the direction of a more directive and active role. You now begin to make input of your own regarding your child's problem. This often occurs when the child repeats the same problem over and over but does not manifest the ability to resolve the question alone.

Step 4: Parent-Initiated Approaches. Here, the parent provides different types of more personal input into the helping process. The following are ways in which you can provide your own input regarding your child's problem:

a. **Parent Self-Disclosure:** A parent's self-disclosure comes after a relationship has been built on understanding the child's problem. Self-disclosure is based on your being genuine and real, and letting your child know how you feel. You may make a choice to share a similar problem you have experienced and explain how you handled it. It may serve as a guide to the child on how to deal with his problem. As a result of your self-disclosure, a child often feels that he is not alone; someone else has gone through the same situation. Self-disclosure at this time not only can help your child with a problem, but also bring parent and child closer together.

b. **Typical Helping Responses:** After listening for some time, you may use some of the typical helping responses previously discussed, with success. Most often, when advice, support, or logic are used and are not effective, they are premature and thus are not helpful to the child. A child is not likely to be able to focus upon a problem logically until his need to vent feelings has been properly handled. However, after you have facilitatively listened, these same responses are often acceptable and effective. Remember to listen for the clues when you use these responses, to verify that they are helpful.

c. **Brainstorming:** Brainstorming refers to both parent and child generating possible solutions to the problem. The goal is not to evaluate solutions but just to gather as many as possible. Often this process can become quite creative; the child can then select one or more solutions to be implemented.

As a result of Step 4, whether by parent self-disclosure, by the typical helping responses, or by brainstorming, the child may more realistically arrive at a decision or solution to the problem.

Step 5: Facilitative Listening. After you have initiated the more direct action approaches (self-disclosure, typical helping responses, brainstorming), it is important to move back to Facilitative Listening (Step 2) to understand how the child feels about your input or to handle resistance to your ideas. It is important, however, for you to demonstrate that you HEAR how the child feels, for your expressed understanding can often be crucial to your child's sense of worth and his confidence in problem-solving. You can also summarize all you have heard and put an emphasis on the solution the child has selected. Again, the goal is to help clarify and crystallize the child's thoughts and feelings about what has gone on for him.

Step 6: Implementation and Follow-up. Implementation and follow-up refer to how a specific solution, decided on by the child, can be implemented. Discussion may focus on practical considerations which need to be taken into account. Follow-up refers to making arrangements for further contact to see what has come about.

B. Example

The following example illustrates the helping process paradigm. In this example, a fourteen year old girl and her mother follow through the six steps.

Daughter: (Comes home after school looking very unhappy. Slumps down in a chair.)

Mother: (Mother puts away what she is doing and sits opposite her daughter. She decides to try acting as a helper for her daughter.) "You sure look unhappy."

Daughter: "Oh Mom, I am. I got my report card today and it's awful."

Mother: "You didn't do as well as you expected to, huh?"

Daughter: "Oh, it's worse. You and Dad are going to be so mad at me. I did **so badly.**" (Gives report card to Mother.)

Mother: "You are afraid Dad and I will be angry because your report card isn't what you expected?"

Daughter: "It's not just the grades. I didn't flunk anything but — I usually do so much better — I can do the work, it's just that — this is hard to tell you, Mom."

Mother: "Now let's see if I understand you so far. You are upset because your grades are low and you are worried how Dad and I will react. You are also unhappy with yourself for the report card. But there seems to be something else on your mind which is bothering you more. Am I right?" (Mother uses Summarization here.)

Daughter: "Yes, Mom. You're right. You see, the main reason I've been doing so poorly is that I've been — skipping school. Oh, I feel so bad about it. I know you're going to be mad! You should be."

Mother: "Not going to school has affected your report card and you feel Dad and I will be unhappy with you."

Daughter: "I don't know how I could have been so stupid. Jan and Sue talked me into it and I went right along with them. We cut about six days and missed tests and everything. We wrote notes for each other."

Mother: "Well, it sounds as though you are feeling pretty badly about your actions. In fact, you sound very much like me when I was about your age. I skipped school with some friends and felt terrible about it later. Most of all, I worried that I had let my parents down because they had trusted me." (Parent Self Disclosure.)

Daughter: "You cut school too? What happened when you told your parents? Did they kill you?"

Mother: "Well, I didn't tell them. The school called my father and yes, I was restricted for a while."

Daughter: "Well, I guess you should restrict me."

Mother: "Well, I am glad that you told me what happened before someone else did. I appreciate that. I know this hasn't been easy for you to talk about."

Daughter: "You bet. It's probably the hardest thing I've ever done. Mom, you are so understanding, but what about Dad?"

Mother: "You're wondering how Dad is going to take this."

Daughter: "Yes. What should I do?"

Mother: "Why don't you tell him just like you did me, when he brings the boys home from soccer? I'll get them to help me set the table and get washed for dinner and you and Dad can talk." (Parent Gives Advice.)

Daughter: "O.K. Boy, I hope he's as nice about this as you are, Mom. But I still think I should be restricted."

Mother: "Talk it over with Dad and maybe we can come up with a fair restriction. Maybe the time it takes to make up that work you've missed?" (Brainstorming.)

Daughter: "I could make up all that work if I stayed home two weekends."

Mother: "That seems fair to me, but check with Dad, too."

C. SUMMARY

When your child comes to you with a life problem, you are interested in providing whatever help you can. Perhaps the most valuable assistance you can provide is your actual manner of response. The skills which have been considered in the Listening section are useful in and of themselves, but are even more effective if there is a unifying direction behind their use.

The Helping Process Paradigm attempts to meet this need for an overview of how you actually help a child, by following a step-by-step procedure to help him in dealing with his feelings as well as to aid him in finding a solution to his problem.

CHAPTER VII

EFFECTIVE DISCIPLINE SKILLS THAT WORK

Chapters III, IV, V, and VI have taught you the basic listening skills to help a child when he has problems in his life. Good Listening Skills not only help a child successfully solve problems but, as we stated earlier, the use of these skills helps him meet two basic needs: Relationship Need (helping a child with his problems brings parent and child closer together), and Autonomy-Independence Need (allows the child to be more self-sufficient when being problem-free). Now we are going to turn our attention from Listening Skills to Discipline Skills.

Discipline Skills are important for several reasons. First, they help you, the parent, to meet your own needs. A child's unacceptable behavior (i.e., having temper tantrums, getting into fights, not following bedtime routine, not doing chores, etc.) interferes with you meeting your own needs. It's a frustration and annoyance to you when a child misbehaves. Effective Discipline Skills help change a child's inappropriate behavior to appropriate behavior. An example of this would be the use of these skills to effectively deal with a child not completing chores around the house or not getting them done on time. The result would be the changing of that behavior to ultimately benefit you, the parent. Second, the use of Discipline Skills (setting limits on certain behaviors) also benefits the child. A child needs limits for two basic reasons. First, it helps give him a sense of identity when he is expected to do and accomplish certain things (i.e., chores, school work, etc.). Second, it teaches him to respect the rights and needs of others. So, discipline when done effectively helps a child meet his Relationship and Autonomy-Independence Needs.

This chapter will focus on how to handle unacceptable behavior by confronting the child in ways that are effective but not alienating.

Discipline Skills are needed when a child engages in behavior you find frustrating or irritating. For example, 10-year-old Billy consistently avoids doing his chores around the house. Or 14-year-old Susan is always arguing with her younger sister who comes crying to you for help. Children do things that annoy us almost daily; it is inevitable. How you deal with this unacceptable behavior determines in many cases how you feel about your child. When the timing and manner of limit setting are inappropriately handled by you, you and your child may end up resenting each other.

EXERCISE: Write down 4 or 5 things your child has done recently that you find inappropriate. It is important to be as specific as you can about the behavior. For example, don't say "He's rude." Rather, give instances which illustrate his rudeness: "John interrupts me when I'm talking."

Child's Inappropriate Behavior   **Parent's Typical Response**

1. _____   1. _____
   _____   _____

2. _____   2. _____
   _____   _____

3. _____   3. _____
   _____   _____

4. _____   4. _____
   _____   _____

5. _____   5. _____
   _____   _____

After filling in the left column, write opposite each one how you would typically respond to your child about such behavior. REMEMBER: It is important to write down word for word what you would say.

A. DISCIPLINE STYLES

Let's explore some different ways of confronting children. We will then evaluate the effectiveness of these different methods. There are five general styles of confrontation that a parent may employ: (1) Internalizing, (2) Being passive, (3) Being indirectly aggressive, (4) Being aggressive, (5) Being assertive.

1. Internalization: When you get upset with a child's behavior and your style is to internalize, you are initially UNAWARE that you are angry and upset. Usually, your anger gets postponed and often in its place is a physical symptom such as a headache, knots in the stomach, etc. A common example is a parent who must be around an active, noisy child for an extended period of time. This parent may get a splitting headache. You, as the parent, do not realize you are upset with the child, even though you don't feel well. When you internalize, you are initially unaware of the relationship between your child's behavior and your physical symptom. It is only later that you may become conscious of your true feelings.

When you internalize, you are unaware of your feelings at the time of the incident. When you become aware of those feelings, you may respond in one of four different ways: being passive, aggressive, indirectly aggressive, or assertive.

2. Passiveness. When you deal with a child in a passive style, you respond in one of two ways. Either you DO NOT confront him when he does something that is inappropriate or unacceptable to you; or you DO confront him but in a very indirect or hidden way. Very often, when you are passive in response to your child's unacceptable behavior, you allow your child to meet his needs at your expense. The result of this consistently passive parental response is that your needs are not met and you feel a good deal of resentment for your child.

There are several types of passive responses. SILENCE is one. When you are upset with your child, you may choose to say nothing. This usually results in the child not knowing what is upsetting you. In short, you are asking him to "read your mind" to find out what's bothering you. Of course, this usually doesn't work.

A second style of passive response is HINTING that you are upset. Hints are statements that allude to the fact that you are annoyed; yet, again, you are not clearly stating what's bothering you. One example is to say to a child who is roughhousing near breakable items: "Why don't you go outside to play? It's a lovely day." A more direct response would be: "I'm upset about the possibility of something being broken." In the first sentence, you have only hinted or alluded to what bothers you without being direct.

A third style of being passive is asking QUESTIONS rather than stating how you feel. The parent says to the teenager who gets home late, "Where have you been? Who were you with? Did you have a flat tire?" all in an angry tone. In this case, you are actually employing questions to "legitimize" your feelings of anger at the child.

All three responses are ambiguous ways of expressing real feelings. In general, you tend to act passively when you want to avoid conflict; "peace at any price" is often the case. However, the result of such action is that your child is left guessing as to what upset you, and you feel a good deal of resentment and hostility as a result of withholding feelings. Over a period of time, relationships suffer and your child gets some of his needs met at your expense.

3. Direct Aggression: Aggressive messages are the opposite of being passive. When you use an aggressive style of confronting your child, you attack or find fault with him over something he has done or said. Although these messages express anger or dissatisfaction, they do so at the child's expense. In short, aggressive responses put the child down. When you are aggressive, you may have the attitude of: "I'm right and the child is wrong." A clue to when you may be responding aggressively may be when you feel SUPERIOR or SELF-RIGHTEOUS. You achieve your goal but at the child's expense. When this happens, your child most often feels resentment toward you because he feels attacked.

Several types of verbal responses considered aggressive include: BLAMING, JUDGING, and CRITICIZING the child. All of these responses either directly or indirectly put the child down. When your adolescent gets home late, and you are waiting up for him, an example of blaming might be, "It's your own fault; you are late." Criticism is expressed by saying, "You don't think of anyone but yourself." Judging is saying, "You're so inconsiderate." These responses focus on the child as a person rather than on the specific problem at hand.

4. Indirect Aggression: Another style of responding to a child's unacceptable behavior is to use INDIRECT AGGRESSION. Such responses are subtle or roundabout means of expressing anger. When you internalize, you are unaware of how you feel; when you are passive, you don't share how you feel; when you are aggressive, you don't take control of how you feel. When you are indirectly aggressive, you want to be aggressive but are fearful of doing so; as a result, you confront others in indirect ways.

One form of indirect aggression is SARCASM. Sarcasm or humorous digs at your child is a way of releasing anger without having to assume responsibility for your anger. If confronted, you can always say you were only joking. Other types of indirect aggression include: POUTING, PROCRASTINATING, and FORGETTING. A child may also use indirect aggression. Pouting often occurs when a child is afraid of being openly angry at authority figures. It is a form of expressing anger, and is also used as a means of PUNISHMENT. A pouting parent may refuse to talk to a child as a means of punishment. Procrastination or "heel dragging" is another form of indirect aggression. Again, a child often uses this passive way of rebelling against authority. Repeatedly forgetting may also be a means of indirect aggression.

When indirect aggression is used as a means of confronting a chiid, there is usually much resentment from the child. Over time, this method deteriorates relationships and sets up numerous, subtle power struggles.

5. Assertiveness: When you respond to a child in an assertive style, you confront your child directly with how you FEEL and state exactly what is bothering you. However, you do it in a non-threatening way or in a way that the child cannot interpret it as a put-down. The child must be able to understand your point as well as feel that you adequately understand his situation. In short, when you are assertive in situations that call for confrontation with your child, you are direct, open, and honest about how you feel.

By being assertive, you will not feel the resentment toward your child as a more passive stance might indicate and perpetuate, for you are directly expressing your feelings instead of holding them in. Also, your child will not feel as much resentment toward you as he might from an aggressive or indirectly aggressive mode of response, because he is not being put down or attacked. The result is a better relationship in the long run. In addition, you have a good chance of modifying your child's behavior so it will be acceptable to you. Of the five styles, it is easy to conclude that being assertive is the most effective method of modifying your child's behavior and maintaining positive relationships with him.

You, as a parent, have probably used all five styles at one time or another, singly or combined. Most people have done so. One of the most common combinations is to be passive for a long period, then become highly aggressive over a minor incident. This is followed by guilt, a return to being passive, and the cycle is repeated. Another common combination is to start out by being assertive, but if the child resists in any way you soon become aggressive. Another combination is to be passive and then become indirectly aggressive when angry or frustrated.

It is often hard to be assertive and remain assertive, but it is also a worthwhile goal. To this end, let's look at assertive responses in more detail.

B. ASSERTIVENESS SKILLS

1. BC Messages: There are several types of assertive confrontations. The first is a BC message where: (B) BEHAVIOR stands for the specific unacceptable behavior which the child emits; and C (CHOICE) stands for the choice the parent would like to make regarding the child's behavior; in short, what the parent wants the child to do.

EXAMPLE: You are having a birthday party with many small children, and you have put them in several groups. You are working with each group individually. Several children have left their groups and are wandering around, disturbing others. The BC message might be: "Joann, Mary, Susan, you are walking around instead of being in your groups. I would like you to return to your seats and finish your cake and ice cream."

B (Behavior): "You are walking around instead of being in your groups."
C (Choice): "I would like you to return to your seats and finish your ice cream."

Remember, B, the BEHAVIOR, specifically describes in concrete terms what the child is doing that you don't like. C, the CHOICE, refers to what you want the child to do, how you want him to change his behavior. It is stated as your choice or what you as the parent choose, and it is made as a REQUEST, not as a DEMAND.

2. ABC Messages: A stronger assertive message is an ABC message where FEELINGS about the unacceptable behavior are added as an important element of the message:

A (Affect): State how you feel.
B (Behavior): State the specific behavior of the child which is unacceptable.
C (Choice): State your choice; what you want the child to do.

EXAMPLE: Your 16-year-old daughter has the family car and is late picking you up to go shopping. An ABC assertive message might be, "Susan, I am really irritated because you're an hour later than the time we agreed on. I would like it in the future if you would get here on time so I won't have to rearrange my schedule."

A (Affect): "I'm irritated."
B (Behavior): "You're an hour late."
C (Choice): "In the future, please be here on time."

Both BC and ABC messages clearly convey to the child what is bothering you and the effects of your child's actions on you. In short, they are assertive responses because they are direct and honest, but do not put the child down. Responsibility for change is left with the child. There is no threat of power or punishment in the BC or ABC message. The hope is that when the child knows how you feel and the effect of his behavior on you, he will be willing to change that behavior to meet your needs. The following are examples of children's unacceptable behaviors and appropriate parent BC and ABC responses:

Child's Behavior	Parent Response
1. A 5-year-old procrastinates about getting ready to leave for school the day you have to leave early for a meeting.	1. (BC) "Susan, you're not getting ready to go to school and I must leave soon to go to a meeting. Could you please get ready now?"
2. A 6-year-old hits another child with a wooden hammer.	2. (ABC) "When you hit Billy I'm afraid he might get hurt. Please don't do that."
3. A 10-year-old repeatedly ignores your calls to come home for dinner.	3. (ABC) "I get angry when you don't come in when I call you over and over. Please come in so we can start dinner."
4. An 11-year-old complains all morning because he has nothing to do.	4. (ABC) "Bill, I've had it; you're saying all morning how unhappy you are, but it is frustrating to listen to you and I'm not getting any work done. I am sure you can find something to do on your own for a while." Then stop responding to that complaint.

EXERCISE: In the following exercise, examples of unacceptable child behaviors are listed on the left. Fill in assertive responses to each situation on the right. Check the Scoring Key to evaluate your response.

Child Behavior	Parent Assertive Response

1. Jeff (10 yrs) repeatedly has been saying he doesn't like whatever you prepare for a meal and has been telling you to fix him something different. He has just done it again.

_____

_____

_____

_____

2. Mark and Bill (11 & 12 yrs) get into a fist fight. You break it up and say:

_____

_____

_____

_____

3. John (age 7) is eager to participate in group discussion at the dinner table, but interrupts everyone to share his opinion.

_____

_____

_____

_____

4. Joan (6 yrs) keeps turning the lights on and off.

_____

_____

_____

_____

5. Carl (16 yrs) is bright and has much potential but often fails to do his homework assignment.

_____

_____

_____

_____

SCORING KEY

1. "Jeff, I am frustrated trying to prepare meals you like. This is wholesome food. But it is up to you whether or not you eat it. Your next meal will be at breakfast time."

2. "Mark and Bill, I was quite frightened when I saw you fighting. I don't want either of you to get hurt. I would like you to settle your differences by talking rather than by fighting."

3. "John, when you interrupt, I get frustrated. It breaks the flow of our discussion. I would like it if you could wait your turn."

4. "It frustrates me when you turn the lights on and off. Please come back here and sit down."

5. "I am frustrated. You have lots of natural ability but don't do your homework. As a result, you're getting low grades. I'd like it if you could start turning in your homework. Is there a problem? Is there anything I can do to help?"

3. ABCD Messages: A final type of assertive response is the ABCD message, in which D stands for a DECISION the parent makes with regard to a consequence for the child if he continues to misbehave. It is usually employed when an ABC message has failed to modify the child's behavior or there has been repeated unacceptable behavior over a period of time.

EXAMPLE: A child is constantly getting into fights. You might say: "You are losing your TV privileges." At this point, the parent is using power and making a decision about what should be done. It is important to note that an ABCD message IS NOT USED until one has tried a BC or an ABC message repeatedly and failed.

EXERCISE: The following are some examples of children's unacceptable behavior. Fill in the spaces on the right and then check your answers with the Scoring Key.

1. John (age 16) repeatedly interrupts you when you are talking.

_____

_____

2. Bill (age 12) has been fighting on the bus.

_____

_____

3. Susan (age 13) repeatedly has not been turning in her homework.

_____

_____

SCORING KEY:

1. "John, I get so frustrated when you interrupt me when I am talking to someone; it stops the flow of discussion. I would like you to wait your turn. If you keep doing it, however, I am not going to allow you to participate."

2. "Bill, I'm very concerned about your fighting on the bus. It can be a real safety hazard; I would like you to try getting along with the other kids but if it continues you will not be allowed to ride the bus."

3. "Susan, I'm upset that you're not doing your homework; I have repeatedly asked you to get it done and it's had no effect. I've decided I'm going to send a note to your teacher and request a conference with her if I see that you have chosen to put off your homework one more time this month."

In summary, there are four styles of managing your feelings when you are aware of them. You can be PASSIVE, INDIRECTLY AGGRESSIVE, AGGRESSIVE, or ASSERTIVE. Internalization is not included with these four styles because of the initial lack of awareness in the process of feeling management. Over a period of time, all of the four styles, except ASSERTIVE, lead to resentment and bitterness on either the child's or the parent's part. Assertive responses won't always get you your way, but most of the time they do. They also tend to reduce resentment and provide for a positive relationship.

Chart XIII (page 77) compares and contrasts the five different confrontational styles.

C. HOMEWORK

Become more aware of your own confrontational style — with your child AND others. With whom are you passive, aggressive, indirectly aggressive, or assertive? What are the effects on you and others as a result of your style?

Within the next week, practice using the assertive skills (BC, ABC, and ABCD messages) with your child. Keep a record of when you used these skills, and the results you obtained.

D. SUMMARY

See Chart XIII: Confrontational Styles, p. 77.

CHART XIII: CONFRONTATIONAL STYLES

	1. INTERNALIZE	2. PASSIVE	3. AGGRESSIVE	4. INDIRECT AGGRESSIVE	5. ASSERTIVE
DEFINITION	Unaware of your feelings	Aware of feelings but not expressing self	Direct attack on child	Indirect attack on child	Share feelings directly and honestly
TYPES OF RESPONSES	Physical (headache, stomach, etc.)	Silence, hints, questions, avoids direct confrontation	Blame, judge, criticize, command/order, direct confrontation	Sarcasm, pouting, heeldragging, avoids direct confrontation	BC, ABC, ABCD messages, direct confrontation
CONSEQUENCE TO PARENT	Not get needs met	Not get needs met	Get needs met	Not get needs met	Sometimes gets needs met
CONSEQUENCE TO CHILD	Get needs met	Get needs met	Not get needs met	Not get needs met	Sometimes gets needs met
CONSEQUENCE	With no awareness nothing is done; relationship does not improve	Parent resents child	Child resents parent	Child resents parent	Positive, no resentment

CHAPTER VIII

SEVEN STEPS TO CHANGING RESISTANT-PROBLEM BEHAVIOR OF CHILDREN

In Chapter VII, you explored a variety of Discipline Skills. Now you will take the Assertive Skills you have just acquired and with some additional skills, utilize them in a step-by-step approach to modify resistant, hard-to-change problem behaviors.

Although the Assertive Skills (ABC and ABCD messages) are often successful, there are times when repeated inappropriate behaviors are resistant to change. This chapter will show you how to work with these particularly resistant problems. At this point, if you have not yet read Chapters X and XI on QUALITATIVE TIME and PRAISE, do so now, as these skills will also be used in this section.

A. SEVEN STEPS

Basically, there are seven steps to changing a child's problem behavior (never studying, always fighting, arguing, interrupting, etc.):

1. Identify the target behavior

2. Make self-assessment of the problem

3. Establish a baseline

4. Use Confrontation Skills

5. Find a competing behavior

6. Make use of qualitative time

7. Final charting

Step 1: Identify the Target Behavior. The first step is to identify the behavior that is frustrating to you. It is important to identify a BEHAVIOR rather than an ATTITUDE. Example: It is better to identify the target behavior as *John is interrupting people when they are talking* (a specific behavior) than to say that *John is rude* (an attitude). It is easier to change a specific behavior than an attitude or personality trait. So, identify a specific behavior that is disruptive and that you would like to see changed. Pick one behavior to work on, one at a time.

Step 2: Self-Assessment of the Problem. At this point, it is desirable to assess yourself in terms of relating to your child before implementing a program for change. FIRST, you need to ask yourself if you have Facilitatively Listened to your child to see if he has any problems which are unknown to you. Do you have some understanding of why he might be behaving in this manner? If you do not, Facilitative Listening would be a good starting point before going on. SECOND, what method of confrontation have you used up until now (passive, aggressive, indirectly aggressive, assertive)? Has it worked? If not, why not? For example, if you have been aggressive in dealing with the problem behavior, this needs to be changed before going on. THIRD, and maybe the most important aspect of the self-assessment, is to ask yourself if you still feel positive toward the child. Can you spend time with the child in a positive, enjoyable way at times. It is important to be able to interact positively in some area with your child to make this program successful. So, remember to:

    a. Facilitatively Listen to find out if this behavior is motivated by an unknown personal problem.

    b. Understand your Confrontational Style.

    c. Feel positive regard toward your child.

Step 3: Establish a Baseline. Now you want to find out how frequently this behavior occurs. This is called establishing a baseline. You want to get a baseline on two behaviors: (1) the problem or target behavior, and (2) the frequency of interactions that are of a qualitative nature (see Chapter X). The reason you get a baseline on qualitative time is that if your child does not get positive interactions with you, he will tend to do things which are unacceptable just to get some attention. In short, these problem behaviors may be caused by a lack of qualitative time from you. (See Chart XIV — Baseline Chart, p. 86; chart both behaviors for one week.) Remember to establish a baseline on: (1) target behavior, and (2) qualitative time.

Step 4: Use Confrontation Skills. At this point you need to implement one of these intervention strategies. You may use Assertive **ABC** or **ABCD messages, Contracting,** or the system of **Logical Consequences** — the latter two of which are explained below.

A. ABC MESSAGES: As stated earlier, an ABC message states what the parent doesn't like about the child's behavior and makes a **request** as to what you, the parent, want from the child. With an ABCD message, the parent goes a step further and **decides** what he will do about the child's misbehavior. In short, the parent exercises his power. Usually, an ABC or ABCD message is best for dealing with a problem when it occurs.

Contracting and Logical Consequences attempt to deal with problems not only when they occur, but also attempt to prevent the problem from occurring in the future.

B. CONTRACTING: Contracting refers to the parent and child jointly discussing the specific problem behavior (i.e., getting into fights, not doing homework, chores, etc.), and together finding a mutually acceptable solution to the problem. The steps involve identifying the problem, brainstorming possible solutions, making a decision and implementing it. Contracting is a method of democratic problem-solving in which both parent and child work together to find an acceptable solution BOTH can accept.

C. LOGICAL CONSEQUENCES: This is when the parent exercises power in a more unilateral manner than in Contracting. With this method, the parent decides what the consequence is for a specific misbehavior and when the child engages in this behavior, the consequences follow. For example, if the child fights (misbehavior) he goes to his room for time out for 10 minutes (Logical Consequence). When using Logical Consequences, the parent should state the rules and consequences prior to implementing them, so the child knows what to expect when he misbehaves.

There are, then, three ways to deal with unacceptable behavior effectively: ABC messages, Contracting, and Logical Consequences. As a general rule, the more resistant the behavior is to change, the more likely the need to use Logical Consequences.

D. AVOID GETTING HOOKED: An important point to remember whether you are using ABC messages, Contracting, or Logical Consequences, is not to get emotionally HOOKED. This refers to your responding in an overly emotional manner to the child's inappropriate behavior. The child's behavior hooks you; you may feel very angry, hurt, or annoyed. Parents often feel the child's behavior is terrible and that they can't stand it. This overly emotional response on a parent's part can be very reinforcing for the child, and he may continue to engage in the unacceptable behavior just because he sees that it highly irritates the parent. So, when disciplining, it helps to be as calm and rational as you can and not let yourself get hooked by your child.

Remember to use either (1) ABC or ABCD messages, (2) Contracting, (3) Logical Consequences.

Step 5: Reinforce Competing Behaviors. In addition to confrontation of the child regarding the inappropriate behavior, it is helpful to find a positive behavior which will compete with that unacceptable behavior and to positively reinforce this opposite behavior. An example of problem behavior may be a child fighting and arguing with brothers and sisters. When you see the child spontaneously exhibiting the opposite behavior — that is, cooperating and getting along with others, don't ignore it, positively reinforce it. This makes it more likely that the child will engage in the positive behavior you want to see and will decrease the negative behavior. Remember to use positive reinforcement for competing behaviors.

Step 6: Qualitative Time. Step 6 is necessary if you found that you had few positive interactions with your child when you took your baseline on qualitative time (Step 3). You might consult Chapter X for specific ideas and suggestions for implementing some qualitative time with your child. Whereas it is important to implement some qualitative activities throughout your child's developmental years, it is particularly important to initiate qualitative activities with your child during the time you are changing a problem behavior. Remember to increase qualitative time.

Step 7: Charting Behavior. In this last step, you want to test the effectiveness of your confronting responses, reinforcing competing behaviors, and qualitative time. You now chart the frequency of the problem behavior, the frequency of qualitative time, and the number of times you positively reinforce the competing behavior. (See Chart XV — Summary Chart, p. 87, and compare it to the baseline data in Chart XIV — p. 86). Remember to chart the behaviors and compare them with your baseline data.

B. EXAMPLE

Steven, a six year old, continues to have tantrums when he doesn't get his way. His parents have tried many methods to get Steven to stop this behavior. Sometimes he exhibits the behavior for no apparent reason. His parents decide to try the 7 Steps to changing problem behavior.

Step 1. IDENTIFY THE PROBLEM BEHAVIOR

Steven's tantrums. Yelling and screaming, shouting "No, no!"

Step 2. SELF-ASSESSMENT OF THE PROBLEM

Steven's parents first tried to facilitatively listen to Steven when he was having tantrums. However, his behavior was so out of control this did not seem to work. Even when Steven had calmed down, he was unable to add much to their understanding. Next, Steven's parents looked at all the methods they had used to stop his tantrums. Overall, their methods had been aggressive in nature. They had scolded him, taken away privileges, even spanked him when he had tantrums. Sometimes these actions had an immediate effect of stopping the tantrum, but Steven continued to have tantrums at other times. As far as positive regard, both of his parents agreed they loved Steven and wanted to help solve the problem.

Step 3. ESTABLISH A BASELINE

His parents charted his behavior for a week. They counted the number of tantrums and noted when they occurred. They also charted the number of Qualitative experiences they had with Steven.

Tantrums

1. Sat.	///	3	When cartoons were turned off, called in from play for bedtime, refused to eat dinner
2. Sun.		0	a good day
3. Mon.		0	second day in a row!!
4. Tues.	/	1	bedtime
5. Wed.	/	1	refused to eat dinner
6. Thurs.	//	2	before school, shopping with mother
7. Fri.	///	3	before school, asked to come in for dinner, when parents went out for the evening

84

Qualitative Time

1. Sat.   none 0
2. Sun.   /   1 extended time swimming at neighbors.
3. Mon.   //   2 father played catch, mother read at bedtime
4. Tues.   none 0
5. Wed.   none 0
6. Thurs. none 0
7. Fri.   none 0

Steven's parents were surprised they did not spend much qualitative time with him. They found that the swimming on Sunday had been enjoyable and wondered if it had affected Steven's behavior the following day. Further, Steven's tantrums resumed and began to increase throughout the week. During this time there had been no Qualitative time with either parent.

Step 4. USE OF CONFRONTATION SKILLS

Steven's parents used a combination of ABCD messages and Logical Consequences with Steven. They told him he would be "Timed Out" in his bedroom each time he tantrumed. If they were away from home he would go to the car. They also sent him a clear message — "Steven, when you do not follow directions and choose to yell and scream, you will go to your room" — in order to remind him to control his behavior. **(Avoid Getting Hooked!)** His parents, further, decided to spend some time each evening discussing the day with Steven in order to keep from getting irritated by his tantrums and to remind each other to spend Qualitative time with him. Both parents felt Steven's behavior hooked them into becoming aggressive.

Step 5. REINFORCE COMPETING BEHAVIOR

The parents decided each time Steven cooperated with their requests, they would praise him. In the past they had neglected this area, just expecting Steven to do as he was told. They sent him ABC messages — "When you come to breakfast all dressed for school I am so pleased, it helps start out our morning."

Step 6. QUALITATIVE TIME

Although both of Steven's parents work, they made a commitment to spend at least a few minutes in the morning or evening doing something both Steven and they enjoyed. Father decided to play catch with Steven and Mother decided to read a bedtime story each night. They worked at finding other times to spend with their son, such as going to lunch on Saturday, etc.

Step 7. CHARTING THE BEHAVIOR

Tantrum Behavior
1. Sat.   none 0
2. Sun.   none 0
3. Mon.   none 0
4. Tues.   /   1 refused to eat vegetables — timed out
5. Wed.   none 0
6. Thurs. none 0
7. Fri.   /   1 parents went out — timed out

Qualitative Time
1. Sat.   /// 3 lunch, catch, bedtime story
2. Sun.   /// 3 picnic, catch, bedtime story
3. Mon.   //   2 catch, bedtime story
4. Tues.   //   2 catch, bedtime story
5. Wed.   /   1 bedtime story (father out of town)
6. Thurs. /   1 bedtime story (father out of town)
7. Fri.   /   1 catch (parents not home at bedtime)

Competing Behaviors
1. Sat.   /   1 praised for coming in at bedtime
2. Sun.   //   2 praised for doing well at catch and listening to bedtime story
3. Mon.   /   1 praised for letting sister watch her TV show
4. Tues.   none 0
5. Wed.   none 0
6. Thurs. /   1 praised for coming in for dinner when called
7. Fri.   none 0

This example illustrates that hard to change resistant behavior like temper tantrums can be changed with a planned, systematic approach.

C. SUMMARY

Step 1: Identifying the target behavior

Step 2: Make a self-assessment of the problem:
    a. facilitatively listen to the child
    b. understand your confrontation style
    c. exhibit a positive regard for the child

Step 3: Establish a baseline in:
      a. target behavior
      b. qualitative time

Step 4: Use assertion skills:
      a. use ABC or ABCD message, contracting, logical conse-
         quences

Step 5: Reinforce competing behaviors

Step 6: Make use of qualitative time

Step 7: Final charting:
      a. target behavior
      b. competing behavior
      c. qualitative time

This 7-step process is useful for dealing with problem, hard-to-change behaviors that children often exhibit. Normally, a baseline chart should be taken for a week; then two or three weeks should be allowed for the intervention strategy, and then a final week devoted to charting for comparison to the baseline data. Most of the time, assertive responses will be effective with unacceptable behaviors, but this method works best with resistant habits.

C. HOMEWORK

With a problem behavior of your child that you want to change, use this 7-step process model over the next three or four weeks.

CHART XIV: BASELINE CHART

Day	Frequency	Total	Comments

TARGET BEHAVIOR: _____

1.			
2.			
3.			
4.			
5.			

QUALITATIVE TIME: _____ | Activity _____

1.			
2.			
3.			
4.			
5.			

CHART XV: SUMMARY CHART

Day	Frequency	Total	Comments

TARGET BEHAVIOR: _____

1.			
2.			
3.			
4.			
5.			

QUALITATIVE TIME: _____ | Activity _____

1.			
2.			
3.			
4.			
5.			

PRAISE FOR COMPETING BEHAVIOR: _____

1.			
2.			
3.			
4.			
5.			

CHAPTER IX

WINNING COOPERATION BY IMPROVING YOUR PARENTING STYLE

Up to this point, this book has covered a variety of communication skills which facilitate understanding between parents and children. You have worked on skills which will improve the quality of parent-child relationships by helping your child when he has personal difficulties and also when his behavior impinges on you. Now it is time to turn to parenting styles. The term refers to the methods a parent uses to handle conflicts between the parent and the child. The focus of this chapter, then, is on conflict situations and ways to handle them.

A. CONFLICT

Conflict between two people can best be defined as a situation where each wants to solve a mutual problem but by different means. Each finds the other's solution unacceptable. For example, a 16-year-old has not been doing his chores for the last week due to extended rehearsals for a school play. He feels he should be exempt from chores during this time. The parent feels his chores are still his responsibility, regardless of his commitment to school activities. Usually, both parent and child feel they are right; they find each other's solution unacceptable or unfair. The result is interpersonal conflict.

EXERCISE: List some conflict situations you have had with your children:

1. _____

_____

2. _____

_____

3. _____

_____

It is important to realize that conflict between people is inevitable. This is true in all human relationships: parent/child, teacher/student, husband/wife, boss/subordinate, etc. You can't eliminate all conflict between people, but you can usually find ways of successfully resolving some problem situations and reducing others.

1. Exercising Your Power. One of the variables that makes up how you resolve interpersonal conflicts has to do with how you exercise your POWER. There are three basic methods of exercising your power to resolve conflict: the parent-centered, the child-centered, and the jointly-shared methods.

    a. In the PARENT-CENTERED METHOD, the parent exercises power to determine what will be the solutions to a mutual problem. In short, the parents use power to get what they want.

    b. In the CHILD-CENTERED APPROACH, the parent abrogates his/her power to the child. The parent lets the child decide on a solution to his problem.

    c. Finally, there is the JOINTLY-SHARED method, where solutions are arrived at together; both agree on the final decision.

2. Acceptance-Rejection. The other variable that makes up how you resolve interpersonal conflicts has to do with your ACCEPTANCE or REJECTION of the person with whom you are in conflict. Parent ACCEPTANCE has a three-fold meaning as it is used here. First, acceptance refers to the parent having a positive regard for the child (i.e., the parent feels a sense of trust, concern, and caring for the child). Second, acceptance refers to the parent feeling secure in his ability to deal with conflict successfully. Third, acceptance refers to having and being able to use good interpersonal communication skills; that is, the parent must be able to use the listening and confrontational skills presented in earlier chapters.

Parent REJECTION also has three meanings. First, parent rejection refers to the parent not having a positive regard for the child. Often, there is a lack of trust and confidence in the child. Second, there is also a lack of confidence and security in the parent's feelings in regard to his ability to successfully resolve conflicts with the child. Finally, there is usually much difficulty in the area of parent and child communication. Ineffective use of the communication skills on the parent's part is often observed (i.e., children are not listened to, and parents' Confrontation Skills are aggressive or indirectly aggressive rather than assertive).

So, parents can use one of three methods of exercising their power (PARENT-CENTERED, CHILD-CENTERED, or JOINTLY-SHARED), and also have the interpersonal attitude of either ACCEPTANCE or REJECTION when working with a child. As a result of this interplay between these two variables, six parenting styles emerge (Chart XVI — Parenting Styles, below).

CHART XVI: PARENTING STYLES

	Attitudes	
POWER	**Accepting**	**Rejecting**
Parent-centered	1. FIRM BUT FAIR	2. DICTATORIAL
Child-centered	3. PERMISSIVE	4. INDIFFERENT
Jointly-shared	5. DEMOCRATIC	6. MANIPULATIVE

DEFINITION OF TERMS

PARENT-CENTERED: Decisions are made by the parent.

CHILD-CENTERED: Decisions are made by the child.

JOINTLY-SHARED: Decisions are made together.

ACCEPTING:
1. Parent has positive regard for child
2. Parent has self-confidence and security in role as problem-solver
3. Good communication skills

REJECTING:
1. Parent lacks trust in child
2. Parent lacks confidence in self to manage conflict successfully
3. Breakdown in communication

B. STYLE DESCRIPTIONS

1. **Firm but Fair.** With this style, the parent makes the final decision about a joint problem that both parent and child need to resolve. However, this type of parent openly solicits ideas and input from the child before making decisions. The parent uses the Listening Skills to understand the child's point of view, and many times the parent's decision is influenced by the child's needs and desires. This parent also states his needs and opinions

in a direct and assertive manner. Thus, communication is good and the needs of both child and parent are taken into account. These parents feel confident in themselves and also care about their children and their needs. The FINAL DECISION, however, is left up to the parent. It is important to note that resentment on the child's part is low due to the effective use of the Communication Skills and the parent's positive regard for the child.

2. Dictator. Here the parent also makes the final decision, as with the FIRM BUT FAIR style, but input from the child is NOT taken into account. The parent forcefully presents his position (often aggressively rather than assertively) and usually doesn't take the time to listen to the child.

This occurs either because of lack of effective Communication Skills or because of the parent's lack of self-confidence. Often, when parents don't feel a personal sense of confidence, they rush through the problem-solving process, wanting to get it over with quickly, fearful that as time goes on, they will lose control and "the child will win." As a result, a lack of trust in the child prevails. Power is often used by the parent to carry out the decisions made. With this style, communication breaks down and covert or overt child rebellion is common; child resentment is high when this style is used.

3. Permissive. In contrast to the first two styles, where the parent uses his power, in the permissive method the parent ABROGATES the use of that power. The parent allows the child to make the final decision. The parent is genuinely open to the child's input and ideas, and feels comfortable with the child's solution. The parent uses communication skills, feels personally secure, and trusts the child to make mature decisions. Child or parent resentment is low or nonexistent. Solutions from the child are often quite creative.

4. Indifferent. With this style, the parent also allows the child to make the final decision, but it goes against the parent's personal values. The parent does not really want to give up his power. This style is often the result of a "peace at any price" philosophy. The parent does not like conflict, and it is easier for him to give in than to work out an acceptable solution where the parent also gets his needs met. Parents who use this approach lack confidence in their ability to take charge and deal directly with conflict situations. The result is that the parent often feels resentment and bitterness toward the child. The child is often left feeling confused and perplexed by the parent's behavior. When this approach is used, the child receives many double messages from the parent, and communication over time breaks down.

5. Democratic. With this style, the parent shares power with the child. Both parent and child input are considered important. The decision that is agreed upon is one that is mutually acceptable. The parent who uses this style communicates effectively with his child. He feels confident in himself and trusts the child's ability to resolve the conflict in a mature manner. As a result of the democratic style, both the parent and the child feel good; there is little or no resentment, and decisions are often creative.

6. Manipulative. When a parent uses this style, it appears initially that he wants to share the decision-making power with the child, as in the democratic style. However, the parent undermines the democratic approach by trying to get his own way by indirect means. He can subtly use the threat of power, attempt to induce guilt, or railroad the discussion for his own interests (usually at the child's expense). This type of interaction results in the parent most often getting his way, but at a price in the end, because the child feels confused, tricked, and thus very resentful.

C. THREE BASIC GOALS

1. Identifying Your Style. There are three broad goals in this section on parenting styles for you to work toward. First, it is necessary for you as a parent to identify your natural style of working with children. Is it parent-centered, child-centered, or jointly-centered? Even though you use all three styles in various encounters with your child, one of the three styles probably feels more natural for you.

For instance, if you naturally tend to be rather parent-centered with your child (you like to run a "tight ship"), it probably will feel right for you to be using and improving your skill with the FIRM BUT FAIR style. If you find it more natural to go along with your child's wishes (child-centered) whenever you can, you will feel more natural in the PERMISSIVE style. Or, if you find that the mutual respect balance between you and your child is more readily maintained by "sharing power," you will want to emphasize the DEMOCRATIC style whenever you can in managing conflict between you and your child.

You may want to review your assessment of your parenting behavior and attitudes from Chapter II. If your parent(s) were high on overcoercion and you find it natural to exert leadership behavior, the parenting style most likely to feel natural for you to work within will be the FIRM BUT FAIR style. If you feel more comfortable with others initiating leadership behavior and your parents were high on oversubmission, the parenting style most likely to feel natural for you to work within will be the PERMISSIVE style. If you see yourself as comfortable with working at maintaining a mutual respect balance with your child, the parenting style most natural for you to work within will be the DEMOCRATIC style. The important thing is for you to acquaint yourself with these three styles and decide which is most natural for you. Once you feel more confident in a particular style of parenting, you can begin broadening your approaches. In order to maintain a mutual respect balance between you and your child, try out the other two accepting methods in specific situations where they seem appropriate for you.

2. Be Accepting Rather Than Rejecting. The first goal we just explored was an increased awareness of one's own parenting style. The second goal which we want to discuss is that of parental acceptance (rather than rejection) of the child, his desires, and his feelings. Regardless of which parental style characterizes the parent, the most important goal is to be accepting rather than rejecting. So, if you are parent-centered, being FIRM BUT FAIR is far better than being a DICTATOR when it comes to resolving conflict. By the use of the previously discussed Communication Skills, you as the parent can be perceived by your child as accepting.

One of the best ways to become accepting rather than rejecting is to implement FOUR BASIC STEPS when resolving conflicts with children. They are:
    a. Acknowledgement of the problem
    b. Listening to the child
    c. Statement of parent problem
    d. Decide on a solution

As we have said, the three most effective parenting styles are FIRM BUT FAIR, PERMISSIVE and DEMOCRATIC. The reason they are most effective is that the parent is being accepting rather than rejecting. Again, the key to being accepting as a parent, regardless of which parenting method you employ, is in the implementation of the communication skills you have already learned. It is also necessary to have a clear understanding of some basic needs children have when they are in conflict situations.

When in an argument or a conflict with a parent, the FIRST need a child has is to be heard and understood. Often the child seems to do little else but argue until he feels he has been listened to. A SECOND need emerges after a child feels understood and this is to know exactly how the parent feels — where the parent stands on the issue. The THIRD need is a desire for closure or a solution to the problem. Understanding that these three child needs exist is the first stage in learning how to be accepting. The second stage involves parent and child together following the previous four basic steps.

In STEP A (acknowledgement), the parent simply states that he and the child have a joint problem. For example, a parent may say: "John, in regard to your chores not getting done, you see this problem one way and I see it another. We've got a problem between us which we need to resolve." Step A, then, merely clarifies the problem.

In STEP B (listening), the parent now helps the child meet his need to feel heard and understood. This is a time for the parent to listen to his child's feelings, ideas, and solutions. Skills that will be useful in this step are: Attending Behavior, Facilitative Listening, and Facilitative Summarization (Chapters III, IV, V, and VI).

STEP C (parent statement) follows after listening to the child. A child will be more likely to listen to you once he feels understood. It is important to state clearly and in assertive terms (not in passive, aggressive, or indirectly aggressive terms) what you see as being the problem, and what your desired behavior change is. This lets the child know where you, the parent, clearly stand. Steps B and C may be repeated several times, with the parent explaining his position while also listening in turn to the child.

STEP D (decision) is implemented after parent and child have both expressed their feelings and discussed possible solutions. There are three possible ways you, as parent, can select to go about this decision-making process in the acceptance mode:

1. FIRM BUT FAIR (the parent decides)
2. PERMISSIVE (the child decides)
3. DEMOCRATIC (the decision is mutual)

Once a decision has been reached, the practical considerations of implementation should be discussed and followed up when necessary. That is, the parent needs to check the who-what-when-where-how of the solution.

Let's look at an example which illustrates this process. John (14 years old) wants to postpone doing his chores for two weeks while he spends more time on a school project. You feel this is unfair because this leaves his chores undone and they become the responsibility of others.

In Step A, you state to John that you both have a problem. He wants extra time and freedom from chores and you feel that someone needs to do these chores regardless of his project.

In Step B, you Facilitatively Listen to John and find out that his class project is very important for him and gives him an opportunity to get some needed social recognition from his teacher and peers.

In Step C, you state your concern. You want the chores completed so that everything in the household functions normally and smoothly. You also feel John's request is reasonable.

In Step D, in deciding on a solution, if you were FIRM BUT FAIR you would decide what needed to be done (John might be expected to do some of his chores and family members could help out and also receive his allowance). If you were PERMISSIVE you would let John decide how the problem should be worked out (i.e., he might offer to do extra chores for others for two weeks after his project is completed so as not to lose his allowance). If you were DEMOCRATIC, you would together pick a solution you both could accept (i.e., you bring his brother into it and the three of you decide that John will do some of his chores and brother will take over some for two weeks; then John will take over some of brother's chores for two weeks after the school project is over).

After this, you would later evaluate whether this solution was successful, and if it didn't work you could again go through the four problem-solving steps.

3. Adapting Your Style Toward Acceptance. The FIRST major goal in this section was to identify your natural parenting style. The SECOND goal was to be accepting rather than rejecting. The THIRD and final goal is to be able to adapt your natural style toward acceptance by being flexible — flexible enough to avoid the pitfalls common to each of the styles and flexible enough to shift to another accepting parent style when a specific situation warrants this change.

EXAMPLE: If a parent's natural style is parent-centered and accepting, FIRM BUT FAIR, this parent likes to make the final decision. But when helping an adolescent decide how to spend a weekend camping with friends without neglecting his other commitments, this parent may feel it is best that the youth come up with a solution and thus learn to accept responsibility for his own actions. In this case, the parent may want to switch from FIRM BUT FAIR to PERMISSIVE, and let the adolescent make the decision totally on his own. The parent's responsibility then is to listen and give feedback, but the final decision would be left up to the youth. Here, the parent rightly feels his natural style needs to be modified to fit the particular situation at hand.

When using any of the three parenting styles, FIRM BUT FAIR, PERMISSIVE, or DEMOCRATIC, the parent needs to remain alert to staying in the accepting range and avoid behavior which would result in the child feeling that the parent is in the rejecting range. Your own awareness of how you and your child feel is your best guide for adapting your style of acceptance. If you feel like "God" and your child feels like the "Devil," you are probably not in the accepting range.

A. Adapting the FIRM BUT FAIR style: When using this parenting style, the possibility of sliding into an overdirective role and neglecting the child's Autonomy Needs is the most likely direction of possible imbalance. This is where your communication skills are most essential. Only through the successful use of Facilitative Listening and Facilitative Summarization will you be able to be aware of exactly what is "going on" with your child. Through the use of these skills, you will understand how your parenting style relates to your child's basic needs. When his Autonomy Needs are being thwarted excessively, the child usually begins resisting in some form. This resistance often leads to the loss of achievement because the child is so busy resisting that his Achievement Needs are neglected. When a parent becomes overcoercive he is usually demanding and expecting too much from the child. This leads to problems in the area of perfectionism, and both overcoercion and perfectionism frustrate the Achievement Needs.

When you find your efforts to be "firm" are not felt to be "fair" by your child, you may not be accepting as far as the focus of the child upon his particular wish. However, as parent, your focus is upon the child's wish in a broader context which you can perceive. So your firmness still may be most appropriate, and by practicing your Communication Skills you and your child can weather the conflict satisfactorily. It is staying out of the accepting range too long that can damage the relationship. As parents, we need to remember that a child may quickly learn to use a cry such as "not fair" to get us to give in to his wishes, against our best judgment. Parent judgment, fallible as it may be, is superior to a child's judgment because the parent has had more experience from which to learn and develop a broader grasp of the probable consequences of a particular child behavior. However, your child remains his own authority in regard to what he perceives and feels. Your awareness of and acceptance of these feelings is what will enable you continually to move toward the accepting style of parenting.

B. Adapting the PERMISSIVE style: When using the PERMISSIVE style, there always exists the possibility of your entering into the OVERSUBMISSIVE parenting role, and becoming indifferent to the child. When you say to him that he can decide for himself whether or not he wants to go with you, and you do not really feel permissive, a double message is in process. The fact that you want to meet your own needs will be discovered if the child decides the "wrong way." When he decides NOT to go when you WANTED him to and you then attempt to convince him to go ("Oh, come on, after all that I have done for you today?"...), the child is likely to react negatively and elicit guilt feelings from you for not being "straight" with him in the first place. This can lead to parent oversubmissive behavior which interferes with the Autonomy Needs of both you and your child. Again, when the Autonomy Needs are frequently frustrated, Achievement Needs are also affected. Parent OVERSUBMISSION results in the child not developing the inner controls necessary for solid achievement.

C. Adapting the DEMOCRATIC style: This style often takes more time and effort than either the PERMISSIVE or the FIRM BUT FAIR style. For this reason, many parents do not consistently use this style. In fact, their flexibility usually leads them to use the style most suited to the situation at hand. For instance, if time is of the essence, a FIRM BUT FAIR method is probably more suitable for deciding who gets to ride in the front seat on the way to the theater. But when your 9-year-old child receives a sizable gift of money for his birthday, the PERMISSIVE method may be used in helping the child choose between various acceptable ways of using the money. The permissive parenting method does not mean non-involvement on the parent's part. The parent in this instance may start with an idea session of the various ways in which the child may manage or spend the money. If any of them are unwise (i.e., buying $25.00 worth of bubble gum), the parent pulls rank and declares it unacceptable. But within the range of acceptable ways, the child is guided in exploration and allowed to decide.

The PERMISSIVE style often involves first the parent setting boundaries and allowing the child to choose within that range. Sometimes the range can be rather narrow, like allowing the child to choose among brown bread, whole wheat bread or no bread for his sandwich (brown and whole wheat being the only bread available). The parent using this style needs to be honestly flexible enough to give the child a true range of choices.

The DEMOCRATIC method most often comes into use when deciding upon events that involve both parent and child or all members of the family. This can involve such decisions as where to go for a family vacation or an afternoon. In arriving at decisions in a democratic manner, Listening and Communicating Skills are again crucial. Any use of "should" or "you ought to" or "you don't want to" is a form of manipulation. Each person needs to have an opportunity to say what he would like, free from any parental judgments such as "only babies would want to do that." Trying to instill guilt in the child is a common form of manipulation parents fall into, in the guise of being

DEMOCRATIC. "What will people think" is a typical preface to guilt-induced manipulation. The parent using a democratic style needs to be ready to quickly and briefly become firm but fair whenever belittlement, humiliation, or the instilling of guilt enters into the democratic decision-making process. Acting as a FIRM BUT FAIR referee, a parent stops such manipulative games.

D. SUMMARY

In summary, your parenting style is very important. Remember:

1. Identify your own natural parent style (parent-centered, child-centered, jointly-shared).

2. Be accepting rather than rejecting, by using your Communication Skills and the four steps of problem-solving.

3. Be flexible in adapting your style toward acceptance and shifting to another style when a specific situation warrants the change.

E. HOMEWORK

Become more aware of what style of leadership you display. Once you have decided, determine what makes it effective. For example, if you are parent-centered: when effective, you are FIRM BUT FAIR; when ineffective, you are a "DICTATOR."

What does it take for you to move from DICTATOR to FIRM BUT FAIR? How can you keep yourself in the accepting mode?

Practice using your style of leadership to resolve some parent-child conflicts. Use the four problem-solving steps outlined.

CHAPTER X

QUALITATIVE TIME — HOW TO ENJOY YOUR CHILDREN

Up to this point, the skills you have been learning (i.e., Listening Skills, Discipline Skills, and Parenting Styles) have helped you deal with problem areas — either yours or your child's. This chapter will deal with those times when neither parent nor child has a problem. This is defined as conflict-free time. This section will specifically discuss ways in which parents and children spend enjoyable time when there are no problems in their lives. It presents ways to help you meet your Play-Fun Need. A relationship is defined as being conflict-free if:

1. Neither parent nor child experiences any difficulty in their personal life (i.e., each is not bored, sad, depressed, or upset).

2. Both parent and child find the other's behavior acceptable (i.e., what they are doing bothers neither nor interferes with the other's meeting his needs).

In short, conflict-free time occurs when neither has a problem and both feel good about themselves and each other.

A. TYPES OF CONFLICT-FREE TIME

There are three different types of time parents and children spend with each other when there are no problems and they are attempting to meet their Play-Fun Need. These are: **individual time, qualitative time,** and **diffused time.**

1. Individual Time

Individual time refers to the times when both parent and child are by themselves, separate from each other. It is time alone, away from other people, spent by oneself, engaging in activities that are enjoyable, relaxing, and rewarding. This time is structured differently by each person. For a parent, some examples might be reading a book, going for a walk, engaging in a craft, having a coffee break. For a child, some examples might be daydreaming, drawing, recreational reading, jogging, etc. Individual time activities can run the gamut from just plain fun and recreation to something involving personal growth and self-fulfillment. The significant aspect of individual time is that both parent and child meet their needs for time alone in a way which satisfies each one.

The main characteristics of individual time are:

1. Both parent and child meet and fulfill their own needs, separately from one another.

2. There is little or no parent-child contact during this time.

3. This lack of contact between parent and child is acceptable to both.

The major benefit of individual time is that there is an opportunity to do things alone, without interference. This is an opportunity to avoid interaction with other people. Since much of life is spent in complex human interactions, momentarily retiring from this process can be enjoyable and regenerative in nature. Also, one can get acquainted or reacquainted with oneself. Engaging in adequate amounts of individual time meets a basic need to understand oneself, to process the day's activities, to enjoy oneself, to relax. Often, we do not provide many opportunities for parents or children to engage in individual time.

It appears that getting adequate amounts of individual time is necessary for our mental wellbeing. When people don't have enough individual time, they may begin to feel tense, unable to relax, or overwhelmed by occurrences in the environment. Also, insufficient time alone may result in increased impatience, irritation, or anger at others. Finally, lack of individual time for solitude and self-reflection may minimize the opportunity to get to know oneself. The first exercise which follows will help you discover what things you like to do alone.

EXERCISE 1: List eight things you currently enjoy doing alone:

1. _____   5. _____

2. _____   6. _____

3. _____   7. _____

4. _____   8. _____

Do you think you are getting enough individual time for those activities? (circle one):   yes   no

How much more would you like? _____

List some feasible ways you would like to spend your individual time but have not tried or done lately:

1. _____

2. _____

3. _____

4. _____

5. _____

6. _____

Now take at least 2 of the above responses and describe the steps you would need to take, to make them more a part of your life.

1. _____

_____

_____

2. _____

_____

_____

EXERCISE 2: This exercise is to help you understand how your children view being alone. You may want to do this exercise with your child. List 8 things your child might enjoy doing alone.

1. _____   5. _____

2. _____   6. _____

3. _____   7. _____

4. _____   8. _____

Does your child get many opportunities to do these things at home? (circle one)   yes   no

How much time would they like? _____

Make a list of feasible ways your child might spend individual time:

1. _____   5. _____

2. _____   6. _____

3. _____   7. _____

4. _____   8. _____

Now take two of the responses from the above two lists, and describe the steps you would need to make them part of your child's life.

1. _____

_____

_____

2. _____

_____

_____

Remember, individual time is something both parents and children need on a regular basis.

2. Qualitative Time

Whereas individual time provides for one's need for solitude, or personal growth and enjoyment ALONE, qualitative time meets the needs of parents and children for TOGETHERNESS. It is a time wherein they interact with each other in a positive, enjoyable way. In short, it is a time for fun together. The focus here is on the QUALITY of the interaction rather than on the amount of time spent together.

Qualitative time is a time when both parent and child are not only accepting of one another but are also truly enjoying the other's company. To make the best use of this time, it is necessary to put aside extraneous thoughts and to become mean-ingfully involved in the present time with the child. The activities in which you engage with your child are manifold — talking, reading stories, playing games, extracurricular projects — as long as you and your child define the time as enjoyable and comfortable to both of you. The main characteristics of qualitative time are:

However, there are times when this way of relating becomes unsatisfactory for either you or the child. For example, a parent is talking to one child and simultaneously responding to other children. The parent is not totally involved with any one child, and this can finally get annoying and frustrating. Quite often in a particular interaction, you may not be in total contact or be totally involved with the other person. This can become unsatisfactory when either one or both individuals feel a need for more complete communication. When either a parent's or a child's needs are not met, that specific interaction leaves the conflict-free time area.

The main characteristics of diffused time are:

a. The parent and the child are interacting.

b. Either parent or child (or both) are engaged in two or more activities simultaneously.

c. As a result, the involvement with one another is partial.

d. This may be acceptable or unacceptable to both.

EXERCISE 4: List five times in the past weeks when you engaged in diffused time.

1. _____

_____

2. _____

_____

3. _____

_____

4. _____

_____

5. _____

_____

How did you feel about each of these times? Rate each using the following scale.

	Did not like	Neutral	Liked
1.			
2.			
3.			
4.			
5.			

Could any of the above instances of diffused time have been changed to either individual or qualitative time? If so, how?

_____

_____

_____

_____

_____

Diffused time is one of the most common ways of spending time in a relationship. It may or may not be satisfying to you, depending on your needs at that time. It involves as a major characteristic giving only partial attention to your children and doing several things at once.

Your main goal should be to increase the qualitative time and individual time spent with your children. The result of getting good qualitative time with your child is that a close interpersonal relationship can develop not only in which the child can grow but also in which problems are easier to resolve. Individual time also allows each person to meet his own needs and develop by himself.

B. HOMEWORK

1. Take a child with whom you have had problems and work on increasing the qualitative time with this child over the next two weeks.

2. Arrange the home so that your child or children can have more individual time during the course of the day.

3. Discuss the concepts of qualitative time, individual time, and diffused time with your children and get their ideas and input on these concepts.

CHAPTER XI

USING PRAISE TO GET BETTER RESULTS

Telling a child that you like him, giving a compliment, praising him for behavior you like, is an important skill for a parent. A child looks upon his parents as authorities and usually the parents' praise means a great deal to his self-esteem and motivation.

EXERCISE 1: List some compliments you have given your child over the last few weeks.

1. _____

2. _____

3. _____

4. _____

Many people, including parents, have great difficulty in giving praise. Often a parent's praise is ignored or rejected, which makes parents more cautious about using praise in the future. To understand why a child sometimes rejects praise, you must recognize that there are two important aspects to praise: WHEN to praise, and HOW to praise a child.

A. WHEN TO PRAISE

There are three times when you can give a child a compliment:

1. When a child is expressing a personal problem. For example, a child says, "I hate school, I'm doing terribly." or, "I am not beautiful like other girls." The use of praise with a child who makes such statements is to hopefully make the child feel better. For example, the parent might say, "You're not doing so bad — you got passing marks, which is good." or, "You're a good-looking girl, as good-looking as any other in the neighborhood." (This area was covered in Chapter IV.)

2.   When a child has no problems in his life and you assume he feels all right about himself, often he is engaged in "on-task" behaviors which the parent rewards with praise. A child does all of her homework on time, and you respond, "Fantastic, I'm glad to see you're getting this homework finished on time."

3.   When the child's behavior is annoying or upsetting to you, the parent may use praise to soften the blow of criticism which will follow.

Of these three times (child has problem, no problem, parent has problem with child's behavior), the only time to appropriately use praise is when there is no problem. If you try to praise a child as a way of helping him feel better when there is a problem, the child usually resents it. In this situation, the child feels you are not hearing, listening, or understanding how he feels. For example, to the child who feels unattractive, you say, "You look great, you're really attractive." Chances are that the child will feel UNHEARD. In essence, you are rejecting how he feels at the moment. This can end in an argument rather than in the child accepting the compliment. If the child has a problem, don't use praise — use Facilitative Listening Skills (Chapter IV), unless you get clues that your praise is accepted.

If you try to compliment a child when you are upset with his behavior, you will find this doesn't work either. This is often called the "sandwich punch." You praise a little, to soften the blow of the coming criticism; then you follow the criticism with another dab of praise. A common example is a parent who is upset with a child's low performance on homework assignments. "Brenda, you've been doing great assignments in class, the teacher says (praise), but you have been very negligent on your homework assignments, and I don't like that (criticism); other than that, keep up the good work (praise)." This type of praise-criticism-praise often backfires with children who then feel manipulated and "set up." If you want to criticize a child, do it straight out and assertively (Chapter VII). Don't muddy the water with inappropriate praise.

The only time to praise a child is when you feel good about him and he feels good about himself. Praise when there are no problems increases the likelihood that your praise will be AC-CEPTED by the child and that it will have a positive impact.

B. HOW TO PRAISE

You know when to praise, but do you know the best way to express yourself? How do you give an effective compliment? You can praise a child two ways: using EVALUATION or using FEELING praise. Evaluation praise is a way of praising that judges the child in some way as a person. For example, you may say: "You look great in that outfit," or "You are a very talented painter," or "You are very bright, you have a great future ahead of you." These messages evaluate the child as a person. They do not communicate what you are feeling about the child. Research shows that evaluative praise often turns people off because they like to make their OWN evaluations of themselves. They don't like others to judge them.

On the other hand, feeling praise shares more directly how you feel as a person rather than how you judge the child. Examples: "I really like that dress," "I enjoy your style of painting," "I respect your intelligence; I feel you have a bright future." Feeling praise shares the "real" you with the child. It is a more intimate type of praise. It does not evaluate the child as a person, so children tend to respond less guardedly to feeling praise.

Some of the results of using feeling praise are that a child feels good about himself; it enhances his self-concept. It also reinforces behavior which the parent would like to see more frequently. Finally, it can help build a positive relationship between the parent and the child. So, praise when NO ONE HAS A PROBLEM. Praise FREQUENTLY, and praise GENUINELY.

C. **HOMEWORK**

1. Praise one child 2, 3, or 4 times this week, using feeling praise. What is the effect?

2. Share a positive feeling about someone that you have felt for a long time but have not told that person. Use feeling praise.

D. **ACCEPTING PRAISE**

We see how important it is for a parent to give praise to a child, but it is also important for parents to be able to accept praise from their child and from others. Often people have difficulty accepting compliments. A child or a friend compliments you on your looks or something else; often such praise causes embarrassment rather than personal gratification. Why is this?

Most often, people feel they don't have the right to enjoy a compliment because they think they ought to be humble. However, when you are assertive, it is your right to openly accept and enjoy the other's compliment. REMEMBER, if you don't acknowledge and accept praise, thanking others when they give it, they will stop praising you because they will not be reinforced for such behavior.

EXERCISE 2: List some compliments children or others have given you in the last few weeks.

1. _____

2. _____

3. _____

4. _____

Now list how you responded to this praise. What did you say, how did you feel, did you express your feelings?

1. _____

2. _____

3. _____

4. _____

A way to conceptualize how you accept praise is illustrated in the following paradigm.

CHART XVII:
FOUR WAYS TO ACCEPT PRAISE

	Accept	Reject
Active	1. ACTIVELY ACCEPT: "Thank you, I appreciate the compliment."	2. ACTIVELY REJECT: "Oh, it's nothing. I've had it for four years, I don't like it."
Passive	3. PASSIVE ACCEPT: "Oh, thanks."	4. PASSIVELY REJECT: Ignore another's praise.

Chart XVII shows us there are four ways to handle praise from others. The first (and usually the most assertive way) is to ACTIVELY ACCEPT the praise (Quadrant 1). You thank the person and tell them how you feel about their praise. You might compliment them as well. For example, someone compliments you on a new shirt. You might say: "Thank you, I like it too. I really like the colors." Also, you can reward them for complimenting you by saying, "That was a nice thing for you to say, I appreciate it."

If you ACTIVELY REJECT praise (Quadrant 2), you indirectly say to someone that you don't accept his praise. For example, if someone tells you he likes your shirt, you might say, "Oh, it's nothing. I've had it for years, I don't care much for it." Here you not only reject the praise but you also turn off the person giving the compliment — something to watch out for! YOU ARE PUNISHING THEM FOR PRAISING YOU.

If you PASSIVELY ACCEPT praise (Quadrant 3), you might smile and say "thank you" and nothing more. However, it tells the person you do appreciate the compliment.

Finally, PASSIVELY REJECTING (Quadrant 4) the compliment would mean remaining silent rather than saying thank you. You ignore the other's compliment to you. Remember, if you want praise, you have to let people know you appreciate it; you have to tell them.

EXERCISE 3: Here are some examples of compliments. Write down what you could say in each instance to let the other person know you like the praise; that is, ACTIVELY ACCEPT the praise.

"Boy, that is a fantastic speech you made!" (from colleague). Your response:

_____

"Thanks for explaining that math problem, (Mom/Dad). You really helped me." Your response:

_____

"That's a beautiful painting you did." Your response:

_____

Remember, it is YOUR RIGHT to openly accept praise and enjoy it, and to let the other person know.

D. **HOMEWORK**

Practice saying thank you to praise and telling others you appreciate their compliments.

REMEMBER, don't punish others for complimenting you, reward them. In summary, it is just as important to accept your child's praise of you openly and honestly as it is to praise a child, expressing how you genuinely feel. When you actively accept a compliment, both the compliment giver and the compliment receiver have their needs met, and thus both feel better about themselves.

CHAPTER XII

TREATING THE MOST COMMON PROBLEMS CHILDREN EXPERIENCE

In the first eleven chapters, you have explored basic psychological needs, assessed your parenting styles, and learned a variety of communication skills to assist you in relating more effectively with your child. In this last chapter, we want to explore some common problems children often experience and also explore the specific steps you can take to deal with these problems.

The seven common problems we see most frequently with children are:

* the passive child (fearful of exercising his own initiative to do things)

* the "afraid to fail" child

* the super-achieving but unhappy child

* the rebellious child who is repeatedly in conflict with authority

* the angry child

* the procrastinating child

* the child with a poor self-concept.

We will describe the basic parent pathogen(s) that often contribute(s) to the problem — you may want to recheck Chapter II — and then outline the needed steps to correct the problem. Now, let us begin with the passive child.

A. THE PASSIVE CHILD

Passivity in children usually has multiple roots which feed it, one of the major ones being the child's physical background. It is important to ascertain whether the child is physically healthy and intellectually average or above. This description will focus upon life conditioning experiences which may add impetus to a child's passive orientation. A passive child tends to expect things to be done for him. He is not a self-starter. Rather, he expects his interests to be sparked by others. Often, he has been catered to — the OVERINDULGENT pattern of parenting. Early conditioning patterns, such as breast or bottle feeding long past age 2, can contribute to passivity as well as can other parent behaviors such as continuing to dress a child well past age 5. The passive child is often not given any chores. He frequently does not learn to enter into group play activities. Frequently, he learns to read well (a passive form of enjoyment), but he falls behind in math and science. When someone outside the family places expectations upon him (rather than doing things for him as he is accustomed to), he may make half-hearted efforts, but soon give up in order to indulge himself in some other passive form of enjoyment. He may fail subjects because he does not get the work done. He is often close to his parents but in a very dependent way.

When these children become young adults, this history of passivity may contribute to their experiencing much difficulty finding and holding jobs, or panic at the idea of marriage, due to the underlying fears of cutting loose from parental apron strings. If they marry, they tend to get bored or experience marital problems because their mate does not cater to them as they are accustomed to. Some passive individuals have poor self-concepts and attempt to bolster their egos by bragging, name dropping, etc.

1. How to Help

In order to help an excessively passive child, parents need to stop their excessive overindulgence. They must cease doing for the child what the child can do for himself (i.e., picking up after the child, dressing, bathing, or entertaining the child, etc.). Parents need to make sure that their combined efforts are not sabotaged by others, such as babysitters, relatives, etc. Older children who expect to be catered to may need to have allowances geared to what they actually do in the way of tasks and chores. They should have the opportunity to earn extra money for performing special chores. The excessively passive child may need to have all unnecessary indulgences stopped, and a graduated program of rewards established, based on effort put forth. If appropriate demands are made on the child, the passivity pattern will change to one of initiation and responsibility.

The older the child becomes, the more difficult it is to alter this pattern. These children become expert at manipulating others to do things for them. They have convinced themselves that they cannot do for themselves, or they complain if they are required to do so. Passive children may find their needs for joy and fun in play being frustrated. They do not learn enough participative skills, and may become somewhat withdrawn from social participation. Sometimes the "afraid to fail" problems emerge in later childhood because their achievement needs are not met in earlier childhood.

Parents need to provide a structure for the passive child. This structure can consist of specific time-units for chores and homework. The child's TV time, a passive form of using time, may need to be limited as part of this structure. In the place of excessive TV time, it is important for the child to be given the opportunity to play with peers. While the child is at the age of 4 through 7, usually he plays best with just one other playmate. From age 8 on, children normally learn to play in small groups as their ability to follow rules improves. Children who are more introverted may need help from parents in order to develop hobbies. It is normal for a child's interests to change frequently during the middle childhood years, and it is important for the interest to be generated from the child.

If academic problems emerge, parents may be of help depending upon the skill of the parent as well as the temperament of parent and child. If the child is resistant to parental tutorial efforts, an outside tutor is best considered.

Whereas passive children need to have parental overindulgence stopped, they still have a need for interested parental attention, as does any child. Your communication skills and skills for dealing with conflict are all necessary for parenting passive children, so that their needs for love, autonomy, achievement, and creative leisure time and play activities can be met.

2. **Remember**

   1. Stop all forms of overindulgence.

   2. Provide a structure for earning allowance, chores, homework, and limit passive forms of entertainment like TV.

   3. Shift from an overindulgent parenting style to exhibiting interested attention in your child's life, his work and play activities. Spending mutually enjoyable time playing with your child is not overindulgence.

B. THE AFRAID-TO-FAIL CHILD

On the surface, the afraid-to-fail child may appear similar to the passive child in that he doesn't get things accomplished (school, homework, projects, etc.). There is, however, a significant difference. The child who fears failure wants to achieve and does not intentionally manipulate others to do things for him or get others to spark his interest in something, as does the passive child. The passive child accepts with comfort what parents do for him. The child who fears failure feels bad, feels like a loser, and engages in self-belittlement when he fails to do something important to him. The afraid-to-fail child is engaging in a form of perfectionism tending to awfulize the idea of not doing something just right. This child wants to succeed, but his fear is like an invisible prison. There is real joy for this child when he can overcome fear and feel a sense of accomplishment in doing something on his own.

1. How to Help

To help the afraid-to-fail child, parents first need to examine their own PERFECTIONISM and possible OVERCOERCIVE efforts to induce this child to measure up to expectations that are beyond what he can comfortably handle at his current level of emotional and skill development. Over a period of time, the afraid-to-fail child has developed a poor self-image by accepting the negative evaluation of others at face value. This child, then, is very critical and hard on himself for not performing at a very high level of achievement. This child needs parent support, encouragement, and patience. Helping this type of child involves getting him to take graduated steps at a level in which success can be assured. For example, this child needs encouragement to work out a special problem, try out for a play, learn to swim, etc. He also needs to learn that it is not awful if he does not get it just right the first time, whether baking a cake, trying out for the lead in the school play, or getting a date. He needs to learn that "DOING is more important than only doing WELL." Thus, he also needs to learn to set more realistic goals in order to regain lost self-confidence.

Parents, then, need to be accepting and supportive for the afraid-to-fail child, not critical and coercive. Parents also need to encourage the child to take "risks" in graduated doses, one step at a time. Finally, parents need to praise and compliment the child for any small step taken; they must be careful not to withhold affection or love until the child achieves at some super level. As you do these three things, the child is encouraged to get started in participating in activities. Once he gets going, the inherent rewards for participating (Achievement Need and Autonomy Need) are sufficient to reinforce the continuation, so that your initial support will no longer be needed. It's important to remember that any excessive expectations or disdain toward the child will only further entrench the fear of failure.

2. **Remember**

1. Have an ACCEPTING attitude and be supportive; don't demand from the child.

2. Provide an opportunity for GRADUATED amounts of responsibility so the child can go at a slow, comfortable, SUCCESSFUL pace.

3. Teach the child that "DOING is more important than doing WELL."

4. PRAISE any step taken in the right direction.

C. THE SUPER-ACHIEVER

The super-achieving child described here is one who strives beyond what is reasonable, and as a result is not developing properly in other areas of life. A child who brings home A's, enjoys doing it, and is not achieving at the expense of cultivating friends and age-appropriate forms of fun, is doing fine. In contrast, the super-achiever is compulsively driven to do everything just right. Grades, social behavior, weight, dress, everything must be just so, or the child is anxious and tense as if something awful will happen because of the slightest imperfection.

This child is usually reacting to parental PERFECTIONISTIC attitudes which are usually exhibited by repeated and persistent overconcern about whatever the child does. Frequently, these parents were brought up on "conditional love," so they have had a lifetime of experience trying to make certain that everything is just so, including their children. A child brought up under this emotional climate soon internalizes it and comes to feel that he has to continually prove himself to others and to himself. It is as if he is on a perpetual witness stand and the prosecuting attorney is always looking for a flaw. In reaction to parental perfectionism, a child usually strives to overachieve. He does not allow himself to find satisfaction in other areas of life. The child learns to belittle his own accomplishments, seldom gaining any real satisfaction from what is done well.

1. How to Help

To help the super-achiever, parents first need to examine any perfectionistic attitudes they may hold or exercise with the child. This is usually the major cause of perpetuating this behavior in children. In order to avoid this syndrome, perfectionistic parents then need to develop more accepting and supportive behaviors and attitudes. The child needs the parents' encouragement to allow himself more age-related enjoyment. The child needs time to be a child or teenager, rather than to be subtly encouraged to persist in overly mature or overly responsible behavior. Thus, super-achieving children often don't know how to meet their Play-Fun Needs and they need their parents' help and permission and encouragement to do so.

A super-achieving child also needs help in order to stop scolding himself for achieving less than perfection. Being very critical of himself leads to worrying over trivialities and excessive anxiety about perceived flaws. This child needs to learn to become a better friend to himself and cease making excessive demands of himself. Parents can help by being supportive and non-critical.

2. **Remember**

1. Be accepting and supportive.
2. Encourage this child to meet and satisfy Play-Fun Needs more.
3. Don't be critical or demanding.

D. **THE REBELLIOUS CHILD**

A rebellious child usually has lived in a parental environment of OVERCOERCION combined with OVERSUBMISSION. In some instances, the same parent may relate both in an overcoercive and oversubmissive manner. One parent may be overcoercive, and the other oversubmissive. Oversubmission conditions the child to be impulsive and willful. Overcoercion conditions the child to be resistive to instructions or limits. His rebellion often extends outside the home to others in authority, such as teachers or school officials. The child tends to seek friends who are also rebellious. The more the parent tries to "rein him in," direct and command him, the more the child resists and uses devious means to get around limits or overtly disregards them. By the time this youth becomes a teenager, parents feel that they have a handful. Calling the child sneaky or a fibber will only aggravate the problem.

1. **How to Help**

If a child becomes highly resistive to commands and will not accept limits, doing more commanding usually aggravates this rebellion. So a parent needs to back off in some areas, and in other areas the parent needs to become more consistently firm in order to give him a chance to evaluate his own experiences and regulate himself. The changed emotional climate which you as a parent can provide can allow your child to better meet his Autonomy and Achievement Needs.

Coping with problems resulting from oversubmission to the child's demands needs to be dealt with differently. Parents should refuse to do for the child that which he can do for himself in order to alter problems stemming from oversubmission. This can be explained gently and firmly, without criticism. This child does not give up easily. So, when your child starts demanding the car, or says, "You have to do this or that for me," your task is to do an about face and leave, if necessary, in the middle of your child's next sentence. Inform him that when he is ready to talk, you are interested; but you are not interested in more demands. A highly rebellious child may need to be taken off all allowances or indulgences. Tasks with dollars and cents values can be posted so your child knows how to get some cash if he chooses. Cash or credit upon demand does not help a rebellious child.

Limits need to be set only when your child encroaches upon others, particularly you, in order to work back to a mutual respect balance between you and the child. To lessen the effects of overcoercion and its incitement to more rebellion, all criticism and lecturing by you needs to be stopped. Criticism of the rebellious child is often an invitation to the child to do more of, or worse than, the very thing he is being criticized about. As is apparent, PUNITIVENESS is often combined with OVER-COERCION. Matters that are your child's concern and responsibility — such as hobbies, friends, choices of clothes, hair style, etc. — need to be left to your child's own evaluation and decision. Your Listening and Communication Skills are of primary importance in assisting your child to move from rebellion to cooperation. If the child feels little acceptance from you, he has little to lose at that time by rebelling. When children have less to rebel about, they are in a much better position to evaluate their own experiences and learn to make their own decisions about what is appropriate. When the parent continues to try to control the child in ways that are ineffective, the child is kept too busy dealing with the overcoerciveness to have much time or energy to learn from his experience.

Sometimes parents and youth need additional professional help to alter these patterns of rebellion. Coping with your OWN feelings of anger or guilt, depending upon how we react to our child's rebellion, can interfere with altering our parenting style from rejecting to accepting. In some instances, a seriously rebellious youth will do better to be temporarily removed from the parental home.

2. **Remember**

1. Allow your child to pursue his interests as long as he does not encroach on the rights of others. Do not overcoerce him into anything.

2. Set limits firmly, calmly, and without belittlement or lecturing when your child encroaches. Punitiveness usually increases rebellion. Help your child evaluate his own mistakes, remembering that children — like parents — are fallible.

3. Help your child talk about his angry feelings; accept them, but do not be oversubmissive to your child's anger or unreasonable demands.

4. As your child shows he can handle the responsibilities and freedom he has, share with him your good feelings about such behavior. Reward him for this behavior and he will increase his capacity to assume responsibility for himself. He will feel better about himself and you will both feel better regarding your relationship.

E. **THE ANGRY CHILD**

Children show anger from a very early age. It normally appears when family members, KNOWINGLY or UNKNOWINGLY, frustrate the child's desires. Usually the anger response brings some response from the parent, and parental responses may reinforce the child's anger. The basic anger response is simple: Revenge! "You did what I don't like, so I will do what you don't like." Anger becomes a serious problem when the child fails to develop internal control. At first, the child's anger responses are unfocused. He exhibits a generalized rage reaction. As the child develops speech and becomes more aware of the type of behavior which provokes parental anger, the desire to retaliate takes on more sophisticated forms. The child may deliberately break something important to himself or the parent, or he may demonstrate certain more generalized anger responses, such as fire setting.

Anger responses can be generated as a result of many different family situations. Frequently, the angry child is a middle child or the youngest child. Parents may feel unsure of themselves about child-rearing. Their own anger responses or spanking of the child do not seem to help, and they may belittle themselves because of their child's angry behavior. Some of the angry children may have had prolonged illnesses, or were miraculously recovered children. These factors as well as childhood conditioning·of parents can contribute to the parents OVERSUBMITTING to their child in their effort to provide love and security for the child. When parents give in to the child's immature demands, not respecting their own rights, the child becomes demanding and prone to use temper to enforce these demands. Eventually, a parent gets angry when taken advantage of by the child's demands, and thus the parent's irritation emerges. This reactive anger is ineffective toward altering the child's anger-prone behavior.

OVERSUBMISSION to the angry child is often combined with PUNITIVENESS from parents as the parent becomes more exasperated with lack of cooperation from the child. Sometimes the child becomes a target for displaced resentment from the parent due to marital conflicts, conflicts at work, or resentment from a past sibling or parent. When parental anger is displaced onto the child, the child may react in various ways. He may react overtly with quick retaliation which usually invites more hurting punishment from the parent. The child may develop a backlog of angry feelings, discharging them periodically in destructive ways, and may displace them to peers or school or the neighborhood. The child may respond with fear of the parent. He may react by belittling himself and begin telling himself that he is unacceptable and bad.

1. How to Help

To help the angry child, the parent needs to patiently and respectfully look for the cause. The possibility of an organic factor from such things as birth trauma, prolonged high fevers, encephalitis, head injuries, hyperactivity, etc., needs to be ruled out. More commonly, a disturbance in the mutual respect balance within the family due to OVERSUBMISSION and PUNITIVENESS will turn up. In order to regain the mutual respect balance, in this instance, the child needs to experience firm limits without parental anger when he is infringing on the rights of others. This also includes the child infringing on his own rights. Belittling others or self needs to be limited. The child can be informed that the family is here to help not hurt each other. If the child does not stop, he can be sent briefly to his room until he has his feelings under control.

2. Remember

1. Set firm limits when the child encroaches on the rights of others.
2. Give more qualitative time to the child.
3. Follow daily chores and homework time routines.
4. Stop scolding, lecturing, criticizing, yelling, and spanking.

3. A Paragraph on Spanking

Few parents administer spanking effectively without upsetting the mutual respect balance. It is unusual to spank a chronically angry child and obtain the desired result. A spanking is at best a symbolic act. When done in anger it may hurt the child physically, and the child will then feel the need to hurt back in some way. Often the child's anger is displaced. Sometimes it comes out much later in life toward a spouse, boss, or child. Some parents continue spanking because they think they should. They were spanked as children and they now perceive it as having been "good for them." They may religiously believe in the saying "spare the rod and spoil the child." It may be part of their cultural heritage. Changing this pattern may bring criticism from the extended family. In light of mutual respect, "spare the rod" is more helpfully translated to, "spare setting limits and spoil the child." Sending a child briefly to his room or having him sit in a chair for a few minutes to cool down or for a spanking are all exercises to help the child learn to control these feelings so that infringement does not continue. A spanking CAN be part of these exercises. Spankings, when they are effective, are usually educative because they humiliate the child, they do not hurt the child physically, and because the offending behavior is specifically and obviously pinpointed as the child is spanked. This requires calm focused attention on the part of the parent, not angry retaliation. It requires such a statement as: "I am spanking you because..." However, if a parent feels the child needs a spanking very often and is so administering them, they are most likely ineffective, and may well be part of the problem behavior the child is manifesting.

In summary, the use of spankings must be CAREFULLY monitored by the parent, in order for him to ascertain whether in fact those spankings are educative in nature or whether they are destructive to the mutual respect balance of the parent and the child.

F. THE PROCRASTINATING CHILD

In the early stages, the behavior of a procrastinating child is usually characterized by opposition and noncompliance to parental direction. Opposition may be quite obvious, such as the child's refusal to do what he is told, or deliberately doing what he was told not to do. Often the opposition is more subtle. When called to come in, he may say, "I'm coming." Called again 10 minutes later, the same response is received. The parent then adds, "Well, hurry up." Finally, when the parent's voice has that special intonation which communicates to the child that he really does not want what's coming next, he responds with an irritable, "All right, all right, I'm coming." The child's willfulness may hook into feelings of doubt which the parent has about his or her parenting adequacy. It is easy for the parent to fall into the "power struggle trap" with the child at this point. The more insecurity the parent has, the more likely is irritability to become a frequent companion of orders and directions to the child. Sometimes these parents wonder if their children have actual hearing deficits.

Procrastination starts outside the child. Parents or teachers try to induce the child to comply with their instructions to do something different than what the child is doing. The oppositional pattern may start simply because the parent is too frequently exercising control (OVERCOERCION) over the child's right to pursue his own interests. But it may begin because the parent is expecting or pushing the child too fast, before the child is ready developmentally to be able to comfortably comply (PERFECTIONISM). Starting in first grade is one of these developmental steps for a child, and, for whatever reasons, the child may not feel emotionally secure for this step. At times like these, parental belittlement rather than acceptance of fears with firmness can start the oppositional pattern. When the child is faced with chores or homework assignments without parental structure but rather with threats and belittlement for not doing the work, the child gradually learns to postpone and accept the increasing irritability of parents. When the oppositional child is met with critical overcoercion over a long period of time, the child gradually internalizes the parental critical commands. He begins reacting to himself as his parents have done in the past. By this time, the child may be given a reasonable assignment and he accepts it. But then, when the child tells himself that he should start doing it, he reacts to his own "should" as he has become accustomed to reacting to his parent. The child puts off, dawdles, finds ten other "good or useful" things that he would rather do. Not until the deadline is almost there, having continuously postponed the deadline (interpreted as the critical parent) and having assumed that he is about to "get it," does he get down to work. Often the deadline passes unfulfilled. The quality of work suffers when this happens and the child takes the consequences, yet without really benefiting from these consequences, in that the same pattern repeats itself over and over again.

1. How to Help

To help the procrastinating child, parents need to examine the possibility of their being overly directive and possibly expecting their child to be more mature or skilled than is reasonable. Anxious directions and commands, threats, belittlement, and lectures are of no help. The child usually thrives and becomes more productive when "Grandma's law" is followed. It translates simply into "work, then play." The child needs to learn to follow work-play routines. Parents are responsible for establishing this routine and the child is responsible for doing the work and choosing his own play. For a short period, some negativistic children may need simple rewards established for each routine followed without dawdling or hassling the parent.

When the child continues to say, "Yes, I'll do it," and then does not, the child needs more structure from the parent. For instance, if a 5-minute chore that the child can easily do is neglected by him (promised and forgotten), the child can be given the choice of either sitting in a "time out to think" chair until he is ready to do it, or of doing the chore immediately. The chair choice is an example of a limit set by the parent. This places the power struggle inside the child. If the child chooses to sit instead of doing the 5-minute chore, it is the child's play time that is involved. If a half hour goes by and the child is still sitting, the problem is more than procrastination. The angry child pattern needs to be considered.

2. **Remember**

1. Make your communications for chores, homework, bath time, bedtime, going, coming, etc., clear. If it is clear, one request should be enough.

2. Follow through calmly and firmly with the necessary routines for the child and for you.

3. Avoid repetitious ordering, belittlement, and threats.

4. Make sure your instructions are within the range of your child's capabilities.

5. Reward and praise your child for letting go of his resistance to doing required tasks and for his complying with routines.

G. **THE CHILD WITH A POOR SELF-CONCEPT**

Self-belittlement or self-devaluation is the major contributor and perpetuator of a poor self-concept. The "good-bad" framework for evaluating behavior is pervasive and is too simplistic and destructive to encompass the many nuances of individual behavioral differences or situational differences. In the good-bad framework, once a behavior is labeled good or bad, the child too quickly applies this to his self-concept. Labels such as stupid, lazy, silly, turkey (or whatever the current "put-down" terms) are perceived by the child as referring to his total self, not just to any particular behavior in a specific situation. With repeated put-downs, the child quickly learns to devalue himself. Even if the child is labeled "good," he may feel uncomfortable with the thought and will soon behave in ways to correct the evaluation.

Self-devaluation not only comes from the family; it is also inherent in the structure of our economic and educational system. It is difficult for each of us to avoid some self-devaluation in our achievement-oriented society. The typical classroom is a highly competitive environment. Awards are given to the few winners. Popularity is based upon certain standards being met. Those who compete and lose begin to hurt from the improper labels they use against themselves. "I'm a loser," "I'll never make it."

A poor self-concept has far-reaching repercussions, on into adult life. Low self-esteem is perpetuated by many avenues once a child reaches his teens. Most typical is direct self-belittling statements. The child may compare himself unfavorably with others, a most unrealistic and unfair thing to do. The child may learn to anticipate poor performance, making the coming exam or social event very painful to prepare for. The feeling demonstrated by the statement, "I know I'll blow it," leads to distrust in self and undermines self-confidence. A self-devaluating youth often projects his self-criticism upon others. The judgmental thought then changes from, "I AM unacceptable, stupid, ugly, etc." to "THEY think I'm stupid, ugly, etc."

Once self-belittling becomes part of a person's thought pattern, it is far-reaching. It is a major ingredient of depression. Believing that one is not acceptable or capable can lead the person to accept and remain in a line of work far below his talents, assuming he deserves nothing better or fearing he could not handle a more challenging line of work. It may lead to choosing a mate who is belittling or incompatible. When a person feels so familiar in a belittling atmosphere, the "at home feeling" of continually being put down seems at least comfortable, even if not pleasant.

1. How to Help

To help a child with a poor self-concept, the many possible forms of deviation from a mutual respect balance need to be reviewed. OVERCOERCION with CRITICAL REMARKS added to the directives contribute to self-devaluation. PERFECTIONISM may lead the child to falsely assume he is inadequate and doomed to failure. OVERSUBMISSION combined with PERFECTIONISTIC expectations for achievement is frequent. The child internalizes high goals and standards for himself, but does not develop the inner control over impulsivity and the self-discipline needed for solid achievement due to the oversubmission. NEGLECT, the lack of interested attention in the child, can lead him to devalue himself, feeling that he does not deserve the attention he craves. Neglect may also add to the child learning to entertain himself, to give in to the pleasure of the moment, and thereby fail to develop disciplined work habits leading to "I am a loser" type of self-devaluation.

Examining and understanding our own ways of self-belittlement can help us better understand how our children may be belittling themselves. To help ourselves (or a child) avoid self-belittlement takes effort and persistence. We need to become aware of each of the many ways we devalue ourselves and practice "limit setting" with ourselves. In the place of self-belittlement, we need to work at accepting that, at each moment, and with the awareness we have at that point in time, we do the best we can. It is perfectionistic for anyone to add, "But that is not good enough." We need to hold these attitudes:

a. We do the best we can for ourselves as well as for our children.

b. We work at understanding ourselves and our children.

c. We comfort and protect ourselves and our children from self-devaluation to the best of our awareness, when hurt is present.

d. The more we limit our self-scoldings, the less we will hurt.

These efforts do pay off. Even though we occasionally slip back into the old self-critical thought forms, we can, through awareness and effort, correct self-belittling statements and literally forgive ourselves. The good news is that we are acceptable regardless of the neglect, perfectionism, or criticism we may have experienced from others as well as from ourselves. Translate this into helping your child know and feel that he is acceptable to you regardless of his current fallibility.

2. **Remember**

1. Self-belittlement is the major contributor to a poor self-concept.

2. Children need to know what behaviors are acceptable or unacceptable, but they need to be free of labels implying they as a total person are good or bad.

3. Any one or a combination of parent pathogens can result in a poor self-concept.

4. A poor self-concept that remains uncorrected can interfere significantly with meeting all four of the major needs: Relationship, Autonomy, Achievement, and Play-Fun.

H. SUMMARY

This book has described how the mutual respect principle operates between parent and child in regard to meeting four basic needs: the need for close loving relationships, for autonomy, to achieve and be successful, and the need for play and fun. It has provided you with a method of assessing your parent style as it relates to your present parenting, and to your experiences of having been parented when you were a child. Six parental pathogens which deviate from mutual respect were described. Parents commonly have experienced one or more of these pathogens and may perpetuate them with their children. Listening and Communication Skills were taught as an integral part of the Program to help you facilitate the maintenance of a mutual respect balance. The helping process for resolving conflicts, gaining discipline skills, giving your child qualitative time, was emphasized. Finally, seven common problem areas which children experience were described.

Should you be interested in more information and training relevant to the concepts and skills we have presented, IMPACT runs full-length training workshops for parents on an ongoing basis. For further information regarding future workshops, training and presentations, please contact:

E. Michael Lillibridge, Ph.D.

or

Andrew G. Mathis, Ph.D.

7804 N. Florida Avenue, Tampa, FL 33604
(813) 239-3332